SEX BEFORE MARRIAGE:

FOUNDATIONAL CORRUPTION

The Stewardship of the Body, the Mystery of Illegal Covenants, and the Mandate for a New Bloodline

Dr. Philomena Gerald

Dedication

This judicial manual is solemnly dedicated to:

The Almighty God, the Just Judge, who called me to be a "Governor of the Dry Ground." It is by Your Spirit and the seven dimensions of Your power that this message of holiness was birthed. I return all the glory to the Throne of Light.

The Mothers and Fathers in Christ, the watchmen who have wept over the foundations of their homes. May this book be the tool that restores the authority of your counsel and the purity of your lineages. Your tears have been seen in the Courts of Heaven; your restoration is here.

The Youth of this Generation, The "Governors of Light" yet to emerge. To the young girl who is making the choice to listen, and the young man who decides to be a steward of his strength: You are the architects of a new, uncorrupted bloodline. This is your blueprint for a destiny that cannot be siphoned by the sea.

My Future Marriage, A covenant established on the "Dry Ground" of integrity and the fear of the Lord. May this union be a living testimony that righteousness is the only foundation for a lasting throne.

And to every soul currently entangled in the "Liquid Sorcery" of the age: There is a Gavel in your hand. This is your moment to confess, repent, renounce, be cleansed and rise. Your identity is no longer at the bottom of the sea; it is seated in the Heights.

Preface

The greatest crisis facing the modern family is not found in the divorce courts; it is found in the foundation of the home. As I have navigated the strategic complexities of the spiritual realm, a haunting truth has emerged: many are attempting to build a "Throne of Honor" on a foundation of "Wet Ground." They are attempting to enter a holy union while still carrying the spiritual cargo of previous, illegal mergers.

Sex Before Marriage: Foundational Corruption is not a book of religious "don'ts." It is an executive briefing on the **Stewardship of the Body**. Your body is not a playground for experimentation; it is a Kingdom Estate, a sanctuary of the Holy Ghost, and the primary infrastructure of your destiny. Every time an individual enters the bed of fornication, they are not just "having an experience", they are signing a spiritual ledger. They are forming an **Illegal Covenant** with entities they cannot see, effectively siphoning the "honey" out of their future marriage before they even say, "I do."

In these pages, we pull back the veil on the "Mother of Harlotry" (Revelation: 17:5) and the marine systems that profit from sexual compromise. We hear the cry of a generation that "wished they had listened," and we provide the judicial protocol to silence that cry forever. We address the "Liquid Sorcery" that has normalized the abnormal, turning abortion and child-out-of-wedlock statistics into cultural standards that anger the Lord God Almighty.

But there is a Gavel in the hand of the Just Judge.

This manual is a call to **Arise and Wake Up.** It is for the young person who wants to be a "Governor of Light" but has been tricked into selling their birthright for a moment of pleasure. It is for the parent who seeks to build a clean bloodline that the fire of the Lord can inhabit. It is for the leader who refuses to normalize evil.

We are not just looking for a "New Identity"; we are seeking **Dismantlement.** Through repentance, renunciation, and the seven dimensions of the Spirit of the Lord (Isaiah: 11:2), we are breaking the chains of the past. We are drying up the foundational moisture of compromise and establishing a new, holy foundation.

The mandate is clear: **Holiness and Righteousness.** Without these, no man shall see the Lord, and no marriage shall find permanent peace. Take your place as a steward. Guard your gates. It is time to build a generation that fears the Lord.

Dr. Philomena Gerald

Table of Contents

Part One:

Introduction: The Architecture of Integrity

We live in an age of "Liquid Morality." The lines between the holy and the profane have not just been blurred; they have been submerged. In our modern quest for "freedom" and "experience," we have normalized a level of sexual compromise that the previous generations would have recognized as a direct assault on the human destiny. We have reached a point where the Church has occasionally stayed silent, the culture has legalized the abnormal, and the youth have been left to navigate a minefield of "Illegal Covenants" without a map or a mandate.

But the Word of God remains the unchanging Law of the Heights. It declares: **"This Book of the Law shall not depart from your mouth; meditate on it day and night" (Joshua: 1:8).** The crisis of sex before marriage is not merely a social issue; it is a **Foundational Corruption**. When a house collapses, the investigator does not look at the roof; they look at the soil and the concrete beneath the surface. If there is moisture, if there is "saltwater" from the marine kingdom, the structure will eventually crack. Fornication is the spiritual "moisture" that enters the foundation of your future marriage, creating a legal right for demonic entities to occupy the rooms of your intimacy, your peace, and your finances.

In this book, we are going to tell the truth as it is written. We will not apologize for the standard of **Holiness**. We will explore:

The Stewardship of the Body: Why your vessel is not yours to "test drive," but a Kingdom Estate to be managed.

The Mystery of Illegal Mergers: What actually happens in the spiritual realm during a sexual act and how "Shadow Unions" are formed.

The Marine Registry: How the "Mother of Harlots" siphons the cargo of your destiny and warehouses it at the bottom of the sea.

The Protocol of Dismantlement: How to go beyond "feeling sorry" to a place of judicial repentance and total renunciation.

You may be reading this as a young person feeling the pressure of the "Spirit of the Age." You may be a parent wishing you could turn back the clock. Or you may be someone already married, wondering why your home feels like a battlefield of "strangers." Wherever you are, the **Just Judge** is presiding.

The goal of this book is to produce a **Clean Generation**. A generation that understands that virginity is not a "lost relic" but a fortified wall. A generation that realizes that righteousness is the quality of a true believer and should be without compromise.

Arise, Governor. It is time to audit your foundation. It is time to dry up the corruption and build a throne that will stand the test of the fire.

Welcome to the War for Your Bloodline.

Guidelines for The Governor: How to use This Manual

To effectively dismantle the foundations of corruption and establish a new bloodline, follow this **Three-Tier Protocol**:

The Audit Phase (Reading & Reflection)

Read with the "Law of the Spirit": Do not rush. As you go through the chapters on *Illegal Mergers* and *Marine Trading Floors*, allow the Holy Spirit to perform a "Title Search" on your life. Identify the specific dates, names, and "open doors" that allowed the foundational moisture of compromise to enter.

Identify the Indicators: Use the chapters on *Monitoring Spirits* and *Dream Indicators* to cross reference your current struggles (nightmares, marital strife, financial "leakage") with past foundational cracks.

The Judicial Phase (Application of the Word)

The Joshua 1:8 Command: You must meditate on the scriptures provided (Joshua: 1:8, Revelation: 17:5, Isaiah:11:2) until they become your "Legal Arguments" in the Courts of Heaven.

Repentance vs. Remorse: This book requires more than "feeling sorry." Use the **Protocol for Restoration** (Chapter 10-11) to perform formal **Repentance, Confession, and Renunciation.** You are legally "canceling the debt" and "tearing the contract."

The Gavel Strike: When you reach the end of a section, use the provided decrees to "Strike the Gavel" over your foundation. Speak the Word aloud to seal the dry ground.

The Stewardship Phase (Maintenance & Mentorship)

Consecration: After dismantling the old, use the *7 Dimensions of the Spirit* (Chapter 12) to fill your vessel. A clean house must be occupied by the King's presence, or the enemy will seek re-entry.

The Conference Mandate: This book is a tool for **Generational Education.** Use it to teach your children, lead youth conferences, and challenge the "Normalized Evil" in your community.

Building the Wall: Establish the "Fire Wall Protocol" in your home. Use the definitions of **Holiness and Righteousness** to vet every relationship, media intake, and cultural trend.

A Note to The Intercessor:

If you are using this book for a family member or a child who is currently "submerged" in the marine kingdom, stand in the gap as a **Legal Advocate.** Apply the blood of Jesus over their foundation and use the *Writ of Severance* (Chapter 14) on their behalf until they wake up to the truth.

Final Order:

Keep this manual close. Refer to the *Scriptural Warrants* in the Appendices whenever the enemy tries to "Re occupy" a room in your soul. You are a **Governor of Light**, maintain your territory!

Chapter 1: The Foundational Crack

Sex Before Marriage: The Entry Point of Systemic Decay

In the world of spiritual construction, the foundation is the most critical part of any building. You can paint the walls of your life with the brightest "Christian" colors and roof your house with the most expensive "Ministry" tiles, but if the soil beneath the structure is compromised, the collapse is not a matter of "if," but "when."

This first chapter addresses the primary crack in the human foundation: the act of sex before marriage. This is not merely a "moral slip" or a minor mistake; it is a direct entry point for a systemic decay that siphons the glory of your destiny before it can even be manifested.

Virginity: The Sign of a Holy Family Foundation, As the Lord revealed in the dream, virginity is a **Spiritual Sign**. It is the mark of a "Closed Gate" and an "Unbroken Seal" over a family's origin.

The Sacred Guard: A virgin foundation is a message to the spiritual realm that your family altar has not been shared with strangers. It is the "Original Soil" where a Holy Family can be planted without the weeds of previous attachments.

he Power of the Choice: Virginity is a form of **Spiritual Currency**. It is never simply "lost" it is always **traded**. The vital question for every young person and every parent is: *To whom are you trading this treasure?* **The Trade to the Enemy:** Through fornication, virginity is handed over to the kingdom of darkness. This creates an "Evil Covenant" that allows "Marine Spirits" and siphons to live in your foundation. **The Trade to the Almighty:** Through Holy Covenant Marriage, virginity is traded to God. This sacrifice secures the home and ensures that the "Glory" of the union remains protected within God's Kingdom.

The Parental Mandate: Training with Truth

The Lord is calling for a restoration of **Truth Based Training**. It is no longer enough for parents to simply say "don't do it." Parents must be brave enough to explain the **Spiritual Consequences** of a careless exchange.

Guiding the Heart: While the final decision to remain pure is personal, the responsibility to teach the truth belongs to the parents. You must act as a guide for your children, showing them that losing their virginity carelessly is like handing the keys of their future home to an intruder the enemy.

The "No Room" Strategy: When a child enters marriage as a virgin, they are entering a **Sanitized Environment**. Because there were no previous spiritual mergers or "soul ties," the enemy has no "legal room" to enter, spoil, or cause chaos in the marriage.

Psalm 11:3 "If the foundations are destroyed, what can the righteous do?"

The Spiritual Reality:

The "Righteous" Struggle: This verse implies that even a person who loves God and attends church will find life difficult if their foundation was "cracked" by sexual immorality.

The Hidden Decay: Once that crack is formed through sex before marriage, the decay begins to spread. It affects the peace, the finances, and the spiritual health of the future family.

The Divine Warning: God is telling the next generation: *"Your virginity is the 'Anchor' of your future. If you trade it away, you are allowing decay into your walls. If you save it for the Covenant, you are building a fortress where the enemy cannot stand!"*

This is a sobering reality that strikes at the heart of generational survival. When a parent the person designated by God to be the **Gatekeeper** fails to provide the truth, they are not just being "modern" or "lenient"; they are effectively leaving the gate wide open for a spiritual hijack.

As you have noted, **Hosea 4:6** is a judicial warning: the "perishing" isn't always a physical death; it is the death of a destiny, the death of a marriage, and the death of spiritual sensitivity.

The Tragedy of Parent Initiated Compromise

When parents encourage "dating" too early or remain silent about the spiritual exchange of virginity, they are participating in what is known as **"Default Submission."**

Handing Over the Seed: By withholding the truth, a parent acts as a spiritual "courier," delivering their own child to the altars of the marine kingdom.

The "Cool Parent" Trap: The world celebrates the "tolerant" parent, but in the spirit, this tolerance is seen as **Legal Waiver**. You are essentially saying to the enemy, *"I waive my right to protect this child's foundation. You are free to enter."*

The Marine Kingdom's Harvest:

The marine kingdom is a kingdom of **Trade and Siphons**. It thrives on "Illegal Mergers" (fornication).

The Virtual Swap: When a child loses their purity through a parent's negligence, the marine kingdom "collects" the star of that child. They replace the "Prince on a Horse" with a "Servant on Foot" (Ecclesiastes 10:7).

The Siphon Effect: Once the child is initiated into unholy relationships, their peace, their creativity, and their future marital joy begin to leak out into the "Liquid Grave" of the deep.

The Stewardship of the Truth: Our Answer to God

Every parent is a **Steward of Information**. On the Day of Accountability, God will not just ask if we fed our children or paid their tuition; He will ask if we **Armed them with the Law.**

The Duty of Disclosure: In any legal contract, failing to disclose a hidden danger is a crime. Similarly, a parent who does not disclose the "Hidden Baggage" of sex before marriage is guilty of spiritual negligence.

The New Bloodline Mandate: We are called to raise a "New Bloodline" that is unpolluted. This requires us to be "Uncomfortable" with the truth. We must tell our children: *"Your body is not a playground; it is a Kingdom Estate. If you trade your seal to a stranger, you are trading your future to a thief."*

Ezekiel 3:18

"When I say to the wicked, 'You shall surely die,' and you give him no warning, nor speak to warn the wicked from his wicked way, to save his life, that same wicked man shall die in his iniquity; but his blood I will require at your hand."

The Reality for Parents:

"Blood at Your Hand": This is the heavy weight of parental responsibility. If our children perish because we were too "embarrassed" to speak the truth, the spirit realm holds us accountable for the loss.

The Warning as a Shield: Warning your child is a form of **Shielding**. The truth itself creates a "Firewall" in their mind that makes the enemy's offer look repulsive instead of attractive.

The Watchman's Repentance & Reconstruction Decree

"Lord, we repent today for the silence of parents. We repent for every time we chose to be 'popular' with our children instead of being 'Truthful' before You. We ask for a 'Clean Slate' over our homes and a restoration of our authority at the Gate.

"I strike the Gavel and I cancel every 'Default Submission' of my seed to the marine kingdom! I revoke every 'Waiver' I signed through my ignorance or my silence! I decree that the 'Blood of my Children' shall **Not** be required at my hand, for I choose this day to be a Watchman who speaks the Truth!

"I decree that our children are being 'Recalled' from the altars of the world! I speak to the hearts of parents: ARISE! Wake up from the slumber of compromise! I authorize a 'New Standard' in our households where the Law of the Lord is discussed at the table and the Fear of the Lord is the atmosphere!

"We will not submit our seed to the deep! We will not trade our stars for the culture's applause! We are raising a 'Sanitized Generation' that knows the value of the Seal! The ignorance is broken, the truth is manifest, and our foundation is being rebuilt! In Jesus' Name!"

A Mother's Prayer for the Foundation

"Lord, I stand over the foundations of my children today. I thank You for the revelation that virginity is a Sign of Holiness and a Shield for the family. I pray that my children will not be tricked into trading their 'Kingdom Currency' for a moment of pleasure.

"I speak to the hearts of the next generation: Wake up! Do not give your 'Star' to the enemy through fornication. I decree that our children shall be 'Knowledgeable Watchmen' over their own bodies. I break the power of the 'Mother of Harlots' over our bloodline.

"I decree that our homes shall be built on 'Holy Soil.' We shut the door against every marine siphon and every spirit of decay. We choose to build a foundation that gives the enemy NO ROOM to enter. Our families will be Holy, our marriages will be stable, and the Glory of God will dwell in our foundations forever! In Jesus' Name!"

1 Corinthians 6:16 *Do you not know that he who is joined to a harlot is one body with her? For 'the two,' He says, 'shall become one flesh.'*

The Mystery of the Two Become One

The Bible is surgically clear: Sex was never designed by the Creator to be a "recreational activity" or a "biological release." It is a **Covenant Mechanism**. In the judicial system of the spirit, sex is the "signing of the contract." It is a physical act that triggers a metaphysical merger. When you have sex before marriage, you are performing a **High Level Legal Transaction** without a license. You are merging your "Kingdom Estate" with the "Estate" of another person.

The Decay: If that person carries marine cargo, ancestral debts, or suicidal spirits, those "liabilities" are instantly transferred into your foundation. You have effectively invited a "Co-Owner" into your soul who has no legal right to be there.

In the spiritual realm, sex is the most powerful "signing ceremony" designed by the Creator. In the same way a signature on a legal document binds two parties to a set of terms, the act of sex triggers a **Metaphysical Merger**. When you engage in sex before marriage, you are performing a high level transaction without a "License of Covenant."

The Illegal Merger: A Transaction Without a License

When God designed the "Two Become One" protocol, He intended for it to happen within the protective walls of marriage. Marriage is the "License" that authorizes the merger.

The Estate Merger: Think of your life as a **Kingdom Estate**. It has assets (your peace, your health, your star) and it has borders. When you have sex outside of marriage, you are merging your "Estate" with the "Estate" of another person.

The Unseen Contract: You are not just touching a body; you are "signing" into their spiritual history. Without the protection of marriage, you are wide open to everything that person carries. You have bypassed the "Security Check" of a holy union and entered into a binding merger with a stranger.

The Transfer of Liabilities: The Source of Decay

In a business merger, if one company has massive debt, the new partner becomes responsible for that debt. In the spirit, sex before marriage is the **Transfer of Liabilities**.

Marine Cargo and Ancestral Debt: If the person you are with carries "Marine Cargo" (spirits of lust, confusion, instability) or "Ancestral Debts" (patterns of poverty, divorce, or sickness), those liabilities are instantly transferred into your foundation.

The Unauthorized Co-Owner: Through this illegal merger, you have effectively invited a "Co-Owner" into your soul. This person's spiritual baggage now has a "Legal Foothold" in your life. This is why many people struggle with "unexplained" depression, suicidal thoughts, or a "dark cloud" after a breakup the person is gone, but their **Liabilities** are still sitting in your foundation.

1 Corinthians 6:16

"Do you not know that he who is joined to a prostitute is one body with her? For 'the two,' He says, 'shall become one flesh.'

The Spiritual Reality:

The "Do You Not Know" Clause: This is a call to **Knowledge**. The Apostle Paul is shocked that believers don't realize the "Weight" of the merger. It isn't about "feeling" one; it is about **being** one in the eyes of the spirit realm.

One Body, One Foundation: When you become "one" with someone carrying decay, that decay now belongs to your "one body." You cannot separate the physical act from the spiritual consequence.

The Verdict: You are telling the next generation: *"You cannot have 'Casual Sex' because there is no such thing as a 'Casual Merger.' Every time you step outside of the Covenant, you are taking on 'Debts' you didn't create and 'Spirits' you didn't invite. Protect your Estate! Do not let a stranger sign their name on your soul!*

A Watchman's Decree Against Illegal Mergers

I strike the Gavel and I release the 'Spirit of Knowledge' over our homes! I decree that the lie of 'Recreational Sex' is broken in our bloodline! I invoke 1 Corinthians 6:16 and I declare that our children will understand the weight of the 'Two Become One' protocol!

I forbid every 'Illegal Merger' over my seed! I decree that my children's Kingdom Estates are **Closed** to unauthorized co-owners! I 'Veto' the transfer of marine cargo, ancestral debts, and suicidal spirits into our foundation!

I speak to every 'Liability' that was transferred through past ignorance: I serve you an **Eviction Notice**! By the Blood of the Lamb, I rescind the unauthorized signature! I declare that this foundation belongs to the King of Glory alone!

We are raising a generation that values their 'Seal.' We are raising children who will not merge with decay, but will wait for the Holy Covenant! The merger is canceled, the debts are cleared, and our foundation is **Whole!** In Jesus' Name!"

The "Wet Ground" Phenomenon

In the spirit realm, the state of your foundation determines the height of your destiny. As a **Governor of the Dry Ground**, you must recognize that different spiritual kingdoms thrive in different environments. Holiness creates a "Dry Ground" environment stable, firm, and capable of supporting immense weight. Compromise, specifically sex before marriage, introduces a **"Spiritual Dampness"** that fundamentally changes the nature of your soil.

The Seepage: Saltwater in the Structure

The Marine Kingdom is a water based jurisdiction; it cannot function on dry land. It requires "moisture" to gain a foothold.

The Saltwater of the Abyss: Fornication acts like an open pipe that allows the "saltwater" of the abyss to seep into your spiritual concrete.

The Internal Rust: Just as water seeps into the foundations of a skyscraper and causes the internal steel (the rebar) to rust and weaken, illegal intimacy causes an internal "rusting" of your spiritual character and potential. You may look fine on the outside, but the "Structural Integrity" is being eaten away by the seepage of the deep.

The Result: The "Sinking" of Big Dreams

This is the hidden reason behind many frustrated destinies. You may see a young person who is brilliant, gifted, and hardworking, yet they constantly experience a "heaviness" or a sense that they are "sinking" just as they are about to succeed.

Weight Bearing Capacity: God has "Big Dreams" for you dreams that carry significant spiritual weight. However, a "Wet Foundation" cannot support a heavy building. When the ground is softened by the moisture of compromise, the weight of the blessing causes the structure to tilt or sink.

The Softening of Identity: Illegal intimacy "softens" your spiritual resolve. It makes your "No" weak and your "Yes" unstable. You cannot build a "Zion Class" career or ministry on ground that has been turned into a swamp by the marine kingdom.

Psalm 40:2

"He also brought me up out of a horrible pit, out of the miry clay, and set my feet upon a rock, and established my steps."

The Spiritual Reality:

The "Miry Clay" Environment: This is the "Wet Ground." It is a place where there is no standing where the more you struggle, the deeper you sink. Sex before marriage turns the "Rock" of your life into "Miry Clay."

The "Established Steps" Protocol: God wants to set your feet upon a **Rock** (Dry Ground). A Rock is a foundation that has been "Drained" of the moisture of sin. It is only on the Rock that your steps can be "Established" (successful and permanent).

The Verdict: You are telling the next generation: *"Do not let the 'moisture' of a moment's pleasure turn your 'Rock' into 'Clay.' If you want to carry the weight of a national mandate, you must keep your foundation DRY. Stay out of the 'Saltwater' so your structure can stand the test of time!"*

The Watchman's "Dry Ground" Decree

"I strike the Gavel and I decree a 'Drainage of the Spirit' over our bloodline! I invoke Psalm 40:2 and I command every drop of 'Spiritual Dampness' introduced through fornication to be **Dried Up** by the Fire of the Holy Ghost!

"I forbid the 'Marine Seepage' in the foundations of our children! I decree that their 'Soil' is Dry Ground, stable and firm! I command every 'Internal Rust' caused by illegal intimacy to be reversed and the 'Rebar' of their character to be reinforced with the Strength of Zion!

"I 'Veto' the sinking feeling! I decree that my children shall NOT sink in their careers, their studies, or their callings! I command their foundations to be 'De watered' from the salt of the abyss! We are moving from the 'Miry Clay' to the 'Solid Rock'!

"We are building 'High Weight' destinies! Our foundations will support the Full Volume of the Book! I decree that the 'Moisture of Compromise' is replaced by the 'Dryness of Holiness'! The ground is set, the steps are established, and the Glory is manifest! In Jesus' Name!"

The Theft of the "Marital Honey"

In the spiritual economy, marriage is not just a social contract; it is a **Vessel of Vitality**. Every human being is born with a specific **"Store of Virtue"** a spiritual substance intended to act as the lubricant and the "sweetness" of their future union. In this chapter, we identify this as the **"Marital Honey."** It is your capacity for deep, unhindered intimacy, absolute trust, and the spiritual synergy that allows a husband and wife to become a formidable force in the Kingdom.

The Siphoning: Pre-Sampling the Assets

Sex before marriage is not a "test drive"; it is a **Heist**. When you engage in intimacy outside of the Covenant, you are allowing the enemy to "pre sample" assets that were never intended for the open market.

The Gutter Trade: Instead of the honey being poured into the "Sacred Jar" of a holy marriage, it is being siphoned out and dumped into the "Spiritual Gutters" of the world.

The Trading Floor: In the spirit, every act of fornication is a transaction. You are trading the "Sweetness of your Future" for the "Folly of the Moment." You are handing over the "Lubricant" of your destiny to the **Marine Trading Floors**, where it is used to fuel the kingdom of darkness while your own future is left parched.

The Result: Drained of Grace

This explains the phenomenon of **"Married Strangers."** This is when a couple finally reaches the altar, but the "spark" is missing, or the relationship feels heavy and mechanical from day one.

The Dry Foundation: Because the spiritual sweetness was traded away years prior, the foundation of the marriage is "Dry of Grace." There is no "Honey" left to smooth over the frictions of daily life.

The Echo of the Thief: When the "Store of Virtue" has been drained by previous unions, the couple often feels a "Spiritual Exhaustion."

They are trying to build a fire with wet wood the "Heat of the Spirit" is absent because the fuel was stolen in the bed of fornication.

Proverbs 5:15–17
"Drink water from your own cistern, and running water from your own well. Should your fountains be dispersed abroad, streams of water in the streets? Let them be only your own, and not for strangers with you."

The Spiritual Reality:
The "Cistern" of Virtue: God describes your intimacy as a "Cistern" and a "Well." These are storage units for life giving "Honey."
The "Dispersed Abroad" Warning: When you engage in sex before marriage, you are "dispersing your fountains in the streets." You are giving away the "Private Water" of your future to "Strangers."
The Verdict: The Word of God is asking: *"Why are you giving the strength of your future marriage to someone who has no covenant with your soul?"* You are telling the next generation: *"Do not pour your honey into the gutter! Save the sweetness for the one who will stand with you at the Gate!"*

A Watchman's Decree to Protect the Honey

"I strike the Gavel and I decree a 'Sealing of the Cistern' over my children! I invoke Proverbs 5:15 and I declare that their 'Marital Honey' is **Reserved** and **Protected** from the siphons of the street!

"I 'Veto' every attempt of the enemy to 'pre sample' the virtues of my seed! I command every 'Spiritual Tap' that has been illegally opened to be **Shut** and **Sealed** by the Blood of the Lamb! I decree that the 'Sweetness' and 'Synergy' of their future marriage shall not be traded on the Marine Trading Floors!

"I speak to every 'Drained Well': By the power of repentance, I decree a 'Refilling of the Cistern'! I ask for the 'Honey of Zion' to be restored where the enemy has stolen it! I command the 'Dryness of Grace' to be broken and the 'Fountains of the Covenant' to flow again!

"We are raising a generation that keeps their 'Water' for their own well! We refuse to let our children be 'Married Strangers'! We decree that their unions will be 'Lubricated with Grace' and 'Sweetened with the Glory'! The siphons are broken, the honey is saved, and the King is honored! In Jesus' Name!"

The Spirit of Harlotry (Hosea: 4:12) The Fog of Spiritual Blindness

In the spiritual realm, sex outside of marriage is the "Gateway Drug" to systemic blindness. It is not just an act of the body; it is an invitation to a specific entity known as the **Spirit of Harlotry**. This spirit does not just tempt the flesh; it attacks the **Vision**. When this crack is established in the foundation, it releases a "Marine Fog" that obscures the spiritual landscape, making it impossible for the individual to navigate their destiny with clarity.

The Marine Fog: The Normalization of Evil

In the natural world, a thick fog makes "Red Flags" and "Danger Signs" invisible until it is too late. The Spirit of Harlotry functions exactly the same way.

Systemic Blindness: Once you enter into an illegal merger through fornication, a "veil" is placed over your spiritual eyes. This is why many young people remain in toxic, destructive relationships despite obvious warnings the fog has settled, and they can no longer see the "Red Flags."

The "Modern" Deception: The Spirit of Harlotry specializes in **Language Manipulation**. It rebrands "Abomination" as "Modernity" and "Holiness" as "Old-Fashioned." It makes the "Normalization of Evil" feel like "Freedom," when in reality, it is a tightening of the spiritual noose.

The Decay: The Termites of Rebellion

The most devastating effect of the Spirit of Harlotry is the erosion of the **Fear of the Lord**. In our judicial framework, the Fear of the Lord is the "Chemical Treatment" that keeps the foundation strong.

Eroding Wisdom: Since the Fear of the Lord is the *beginning* of wisdom (Proverbs 9:10), its removal marks the *beginning* of folly. Once the reverence for God is drained from the foundation, the structure becomes "Soft."

The Termites of Rebellion: With the Fear of the Lord gone, the **Termites of Rebellion** move in. They begin to eat away at your character, your integrity, and your ability to submit to divine authority. You begin to question the Word of God, not because it isn't true, but because your "Foundation" has been hollowed out by the spirit of harlotry.

Hosea 4:12

"My people ask counsel from their wooden idols, and their staff informs them. For the spirit of harlotry has caused them to stray, and they have played the harlot against their God."

The Spiritual Reality:

The "Caused Them to Stray" Clause: Notice that the straying is a **Result**. The spirit of harlotry enters first, then the "Straying" (the bad decisions, the wrong partners, the loss of path) follows.

Seeking Counsel from Idols: When the fog is thick, people stop hearing the Voice of God and start seeking advice from "Idols" social media trends, ungodly friends, and their own darkened emotions.
The Verdict: You are telling the next generation: *"Do not let the 'Fog' settle on your eyes! The moment you compromise your purity, you lose your 'Navigation System.' The Spirit of Harlotry wants to blind you so it can lead you into the abyss. Keep your vision clear by keeping your bed undefiled!"*

A Watchman's Decree Against Spiritual Blindness

"I strike the Gavel and I release the 'Wind of the Holy Ghost' to blow away every 'Marine Fog' over our seed! I invoke Hosea 4:12 and I bind the Spirit of Harlotry from the foundations of our children!

"I decree that the 'Veil of Blindness' is torn off! I command our children's eyes to be opened to see 'Red Flags' with 20/20 spiritual vision! I 'Veto' the lie of 'Modernity' that seeks to normalize evil in our bloodline!

"I decree a 'Restoration of the Fear of the Lord'! I command the 'Termites of Rebellion' to DIE at the root! I 'Chemicalize' the foundation of our homes with the Wisdom of God, making it impenetrable to the spirit of harlotry!

"We are raising a generation with 'Eagle Eyes'! They will not stray, they will not be deceived, and they will not seek counsel from idols! They will hear the Voice of the Lord clearly because their foundation is Holy! The fog is lifted, the Fear is restored, and the Vision is sharp! In Jesus' Name!"

The Legal Ledger of the Deep

Finally, sex before marriage is the primary way names are "registered" in the **Marine Ledger**.

The Contract: In the deep, a sexual act is viewed as a "Sacrifice of Virtue." The Marine Kingdom accepts this sacrifice and, in exchange, issues a **Spirit Spouse** to "monitor" the individual.

The Hold: This entity now has a "Foundational Claim" on you. This is the crack that allows the enemy to say in the Court of Heaven: *"I have a right to this person's bed because they gave me the keys through their own disobedience."*

The Governor's Verdict

You cannot build a "Palace of Purity" on a "Crack of Compromise." If you have allowed this crack to form, you must not just "patch it" with a prayer; you must **Dismantle and Re pour** the foundation through deep repentance and the judicial application of the Blood of Jesus.

Decree: *"I recognize the crack in my foundation. I refuse to normalize the decay of my destiny. By the Gavel of the Just Judge, I declare that the moisture of fornication is drying up now, and my foundation is being reinforced with the Stone of Holiness, in the Name of Jesus!"*

The Stewardship of The Body: Understanding Your Vessel as a Kingdom Estate

In the language of the Kingdom, your body is not a "private residence" to be managed by your feelings; it is a **Kingdom Estate**. It is sovereign territory under the jurisdiction of the Almighty. When we speak of Stewardship, we are discussing the administrative responsibility of an officer to manage an asset that belongs to a Higher Authority. To treat your body as your own is not just a "mistake"; it is **Embezzlement of Divine Property**.

The Body as a Sovereign Embassy

The Scripture is surgically clear: *"Do you not know that your body is the temple of the Holy Spirit who is in you... you are not your own?"* (**1 Corinthians 6:19**).

The Legal Status: In international law, an **Embassy** is considered the sovereign territory of the home nation, even if it physically sits in a foreign land. Your body is an **Embassy of Zion** on Earth. It is "Extraterritorial Property." The laws of the world (the culture of "hookups" and "casual sex") have no legal standing within your borders because you are governed by the Constitution of Heaven.

The Violation: When you engage in sex before marriage, you are allowing a **"Foreign Power"** (the Marine Kingdom or a demonic entity) to stage an illegal occupation within the Embassy. You are effectively handing over the keys of the King's property to His enemies. By doing so, you are allowing an enemy flag to fly over a territory that was bought with the Price of Blood.

The Charge of Embezzlement

If an administrator takes the funds of a corporation for personal use, they are charged with **Embezzlement**.

The Misappropriation of Assets: Your sexual energy, your reproductive capacity, and your emotional depth are "Kingdom Assets." They were given to you to "fund" a Holy Covenant. When you use these assets for fornication, you are misappropriating the King's resources for your own "emotional profit."

The Divine Audit: Every act of stewardship will eventually face an audit. As a Governor, you must understand that you will be asked to give an account for how you managed the "Real Estate" of your body. Did you maintain the Embassy's borders, or did you allow it to become a "Squatter's Camp" for the kingdom of darkness?

1 Corinthians 6:20
"For you were bought at a price; therefore, glorify God in your body and in your spirit, which are God's."

The Spiritual Reality:
The "Bought at a Price" Clause: This is the **Bill of Sale**. The Blood of Christ was the currency used to purchase your body. Legally, you have no "Title Deed" to yourself.
The Glory Mandate: To "Glorify God in your body" is to manage the property in a way that reflects the King's character.
The Verdict: You are telling the next generation: *"You are a high value asset! You are a Sovereign Embassy! Do not let a common trespasser occupy the King's land. Keep the borders tight, for the Owner is coming to inspect His Estate!"*

A Watchman's "Embassy Security" Decree
"I strike the Gavel and I declare that my body and the bodies of my children are **Sovereign Kingdom Estates**! I invoke 1 Corinthians 6:19 and I decree that we are NOT our own we are the Property of the King of Glory!

"I issue a 'Cease and Desist' order to every foreign power attempting to stage an illegal occupation of our vessels! I cancel every 'Embassy Breach' caused by the spirit of fornication! I 'Veto' the spirit of embezzlement and I decree that our sexual virtues are **Reserved** for the King's use alone!

"I command every 'Squatter Spirit' and 'Marine Entity' that has moved into our territory to **Get Out Now**! I reclaim the keys to the Embassy! I decree that the Flag of Zion is the ONLY flag flying over this bloodline! We will not misappropriate the King's assets; we will manage this Estate with Holiness and Integrity!

"Our bodies are Sanctuary! Our vessels are Secure! The borders are locked against the world and open to the Spirit! The Estate is

Holy, the Stewardship is True, and the King is Glorified! In Jesus' Name!"

The Estate Audit: Managing Your "Gates"

In the judicial framework of the Kingdom, every **Estate** is defined by its boundaries. If an estate has no functional gates, it is no longer a private territory; it is a public thoroughfare. As a Steward of your body, you have been appointed as the **Chief Security Officer (CSO)** of three primary entry points: the **Eye gate**, the **Ear gate**, and the **Gate of Intimacy**.

An audit of your life will always begin at these gates, for they determine what is allowed to "legally" inhibit your foundation.

The Integrity of the Fence

Stewardship is not just about keeping the inside clean; it is about maintaining the **Fencing** of your soul. A fence is only as strong as its weakest point.

The Breach of Sex: In the spirit, the Gate of Intimacy is the "Master Gate." While the eye and ear gates allow *influence* to enter, the gate of sex allows a *merger* to take place.

The Security Failure: If you allow an "illegal merger" through the gate of intimacy, you have not just made a mistake; you have breached the security of the **entire estate**. Once the enemy is "inside" through a sexual covenant, he no longer needs to climb the fence; he has been handed the keys to the main house.

Systemic Exposure: The Silencing of the Alarms

When a security system is compromised, the first thing an intruder does is "cut the wires" to the alarm. In the human soul, the **Conscience** is the Security Alarm.

The Silenced Alarm: Once the gate of intimacy is compromised through fornication, the "Security Alarms" of your conscience are often silenced or "dampened." You begin to lose your spiritual sensitivity.

The Spread of Corruption: This is how **Foundational Corruption** becomes systemic. A steward who fails to guard the gate of intimacy will eventually find that the corruption spreads to:

The Treasury: Your finances become "leaky" and unblessed because of the marine siphons attached to the merger.

The Throne Room: Your prayer life becomes cold and mechanical because the "Embassy" is under illegal occupation.

Proverbs 25:28

"Whoever has no rule over his own spirit is like a city broken down, without walls."

The Spiritual Reality:

The "Broken Down" City: A person without "Gate Control" is not a sovereign estate; they are a "Broken City." Any spirit, any debt, or any disease can walk in and out without permission.

The "No Rule" Penalty: To have "no rule" over your spirit is to resign from your position as a Steward. It is to let the Estate go into "Spiritual Foreclosure."

The Verdict: You are telling the next generation: *"You are the CSO of your own life! Check the ID of every influence at the gate. If it doesn't have a Covenant License, do not let it in. Keep the fence high and the alarms active!"*

A Watchman's "Estate Audit" Decree

"I strike the Gavel and I commission a 'Security Audit' over the gates of my children! I invoke Proverbs 25:28 and I decree that their 'Walls' shall be rebuilt and their 'Gates' shall be reinforced by the Power of the Holy Ghost!

"I activate the 'Security Alarms' of their conscience! I decree that any attempt at an 'Illegal Merger' will trigger a 'Divine Siren' in their spirit that they cannot ignore! I 'Veto' the silencing of the alarm and I decree a 'Sensitivity' to the frequency of Zion!

"I command every 'Breach' in the fence to be repaired! I 'Seal' the Gate of Intimacy with the Blood of the Lamb! I decree that the Treasury (finances) and the Throne Room (prayer) of our bloodline are **Protected** from systemic corruption!

"Our children will not be 'Broken Down Cities'! They will be 'Fortified Estates'! They will rule over their spirits and manage their gates with the Wisdom of God! The audit is passed, the walls are up, and the Estate is Secure! In Jesus' Name!"

The High Cost of "Maintenance Neglect"

In the spirit realm, every Kingdom Estate is governed by a **Manufacturer's Manual** the Word of God. This manual contains the precise "Maintenance Protocols" required to keep the structure standing for generations. When a Steward ignores these protocols, they enter a state of **Maintenance Neglect**. This is not a passive condition; it is an active invitation for **Systemic Decay** to eat away at the very fabric of your life.

The Biological and Spiritual Toll: The Chemical Collision

When the Manual says, "Flee sexual immorality," it is providing a safety warning for your internal "Soil."

The Chemical Collision: Sex is more than a physical act; it is a profound biological and spiritual "Bonding Agent." When you engage in an illegal union, you are initiating a **Chemical and Spiritual Collision**.

Mixing the Soil: You are literally mixing the "clean soil" of your estate with the "toxins" found in the estate of another. This creates a spiritual "sludge" that clogs your spiritual pores and dampens your ability to resonate with the frequency of the Holy Spirit. You become "heavy" with a weight that was never yours to carry.

The Siphoning of Value: The Looting of the Estate

A Steward who allows "unauthorized guests" into the Estate through the gate of fornication soon discovers that the **"Furniture of Virtue"** is disappearing.

The Looting Protocol: As **John 10:10** declares, the thief does not come for a social visit; he comes to **Steal, Kill, and Destroy**. When the Marine Kingdom enters your foundation through an illegal merger, it immediately begins to "Loot" the interior:

Prophetic Clarity: The "Windows" of your soul become clouded.

Peace and Joy: The "Atmosphere" of the estate becomes filled with anxiety and heaviness.

Confidence: The "Pillars" of your identity begin to shake.

The Empty House: If the neglect continues, you will find yourself in a house that looks "Christian" on the outside but has been completely emptied of its spiritual wealth on the inside. You are left with the "Walls" of religion but none of the "Furniture" of the Spirit.

Proverbs 6:32

"Whoever commits adultery with a woman lacks understanding; He who does so destroys his own soul."

The Spiritual Reality:

The "Lacks Understanding" Verdict: In judicial terms, the person who ignores the Manual is declared "Incompetent." They do not understand the **Replacement Cost** of the virtues they are losing.

The "Destroys His Own Soul" Clause: This is self-inflicted **Maintenance Neglect**. The decay doesn't come from the outside; it is a "Demolition" that starts from within the foundation.

The Verdict: You are telling the next generation: *"The Manual is not there to restrict your fun; it is there to prevent your Destruction! Do not let the thief 'Loot' your joy for the price of a night's pleasure. Keep the maintenance up, and the virtues will stay in the house!"*

A Watchman's "Maintenance Recovery" Decree

"I strike the Gavel and I decree a 'Repossession of the Furniture of Virtue' in our bloodline! I invoke John 10:10 and I declare that the Thief is **Caught**! I command a **Seven-Fold Restoration** of every virtue stolen through the gate of fornication!

"I 'Veto' the spirit of Maintenance Neglect! I decree that our children will be 'Students of the Manual' (Joshua 1:8) and 'Enforcers of the Protocol'! I command the 'Spiritual Toxins' introduced through past collisions to be **Neutralized** by the Blood of Jesus!

"I decree that the 'Windows' of prophetic clarity are being cleaned! I command the 'Pillars' of confidence to be reinforced! We will not live in an 'Empty House'! We decree that our Kingdom Estates are FULL of the Peace, Joy, and Power of the Almighty!

"We choose the 'Standard of the Manufacturer'! We refuse the 'Systemic Decay' of the world! Our structures are solid, our furniture is secure, and our Estate is flourishing! In Jesus' Name!"

The Stewardship of the Bloodline

In the judicial council of the Kingdom, you are never viewed as an isolated individual. You are viewed as a **Trustee**. You are not just stewarding your body for your own comfort; you are managing the **Seed Bank** of your future generations. Your current choices are the "environmental conditions" that will either nourish or poison the harvest of your grandchildren.

The Genetic Trust: Keeping the Water Pure

Your body is the container for a **Genetic Trust**. This trust is the raw material from which God will fashion the bodies and temperaments of your children.

The Water of the Word: By practicing holiness and maintaining a "Dry Ground" foundation, you are keeping the "Water" of your lineage pure.

The Filtration System: Purity acts as a filtration system that prevents the "toxins of the world" from entering the seed bank. When you remain undefiled, you ensure that the "DNA of Destiny" passed to your children is not pre packaged with the spiritual viruses of lust, perversion, or addiction.

Generational Liability: Passing Down a Clear Title

In the natural world, if a parent dies with massive debt, the estate is placed **"Under Lien."** The children cannot enjoy the inheritance because the creditors have a legal claim on it.

The Marine Creditors: When you compromise the Estate through sex before marriage, you are racking up **Generational Debt**. You are essentially allowing "Marine Creditors" and "Spirit Spouses" to place a lien on your loins.

The Clear Title: Proper stewardship ensures that when your children are born, they inherit an Estate with a **"Clear Title."** This means no demon can show up at their "Gate" and claim ownership based on a transaction you made in a hotel room twenty years ago. You are giving them the gift of a "Debt Free Start."

Exodus 20:5-6

"...visiting the iniquity of the fathers upon the children to the third and fourth generations of those who hate Me, but showing mercy to thousands, to those who love Me and keep My commandments."

The Spiritual Reality:

The "Visiting Iniquity" Clause: This is the description of a **Generational Lien**. If the foundation is cracked by the father or mother, the "repair bill" often falls on the children.

The "Mercy to Thousands" Clause: This is the reward for **Faithful Stewardship**. When you keep the commandments, you are creating a "Mercy Fund" that blankets your descendants for thousands of generations.

The Verdict: You are telling the next generation: *"You are carrying a 'Trust Fund' of destiny! Do not spend your children's inheritance on a moment's pleasure. Keep the title clear so your seed can run without being chased by your ghosts!"*

A Watchman's "Bloodline Trustee" Decree

"I strike the Gavel and I declare myself a 'Faithful Trustee' of the Seed-Bank of Zion! I invoke Exodus 20:6 and I decree that I am building a 'Mercy Fund' that will cover my descendants for a thousand generations!

"I 'Veto' and cancel every 'Generational Lien' attempted against my seed! I serve an 'Eviction Notice' to every marine creditor and spirit spouse claiming a debt against my bloodline! By the Blood of the Lamb, I settle every account and I declare that I am passing down a **Clear Title** to my children!

"I decree that the 'Water of the Word' in my loins is **Pure** and **Undefiled**! I command every 'Genetic virus' of lust and rebellion to DIE at the root! My seed shall not inherit 'Under Lien'; they shall inherit 'Under Blessing'!

"I choose the 'Protocol of Purity' for the sake of those who come after me! I am a Governor of the Bloodline, and I declare that this Estate is Debt Free, Holy, and Whole! The Title is Clear, the Seed is Blessed, and the King is Honored! In Jesus' Name!"

The Seven Dimensions of Administrative Power, The Administrative Capacity: Beyond Willpower

To steward a **Kingdom Estate** and maintain the "Dry Ground" of your foundation, you cannot rely on human "willpower." Willpower is a biological resource that depletes under pressure. To effectively govern your vessel, you need the **Administrative Capacity** of Heaven. This capacity is found in the **Seven Fold Spirit of the Lord** as outlined in **Isaiah 11:2**.

These are not just religious feelings; they are the **Seven Commissioners of the Estate**, each responsible for a different department of your spiritual security.

The Spirit of Wisdom and Understanding: The Intelligence Department

These dimensions function as your **Spiritual Radar**.

The Spirit of Wisdom: This is the "Architect." It understands the long-term structural impact of every decision. It warns you: *"That 'casual' connection is actually a demolition ball aimed at your foundation."*

The Spirit of Understanding: This is the "Discernment Officer." It looks past the outward appearance of a person or situation to see the underlying spiritual "Traps" before they are sprung. It deciphers the "Marine Fog" and reveals the hidden hooks.

The Spirit of Counsel and Might: The Enforcement Department

Once a trap is identified, you need the "Instruction" to escape and the "Power" to stay out.

The Spirit of Counsel: This is the "Legal Advisor." In the heat of temptation, it brings to your remembrance the specific "Protocols of Zion" required to navigate the moment. It provides the "Strategy of Escape."

The Spirit of Might: This is the "Enforcement Agency." It provides the **Executive Strength** to stand firm when the pressure to compromise rises. Might is the spiritual muscle that enables you to say "No" and have it stick.

The Spirit of Knowledge and the Fear of the Lord: The Compliance Department

This department ensures that the Steward remains aligned with the Home Nation (Zion).

The Spirit of Knowledge: This is the "Evidence Ledger." It provides you with the facts of the Spirit Realm reminding you of the reality of covenants, siphons, and the "Genetic Trust" you are carrying.

The Spirit of the Fear of the Lord: This is the "Chief Auditor." It is the constant, holy awareness that the **Owner of the Estate** is watching the management. It creates a reverence that makes "Embezzlement" (using the body for sin) an unthinkable crime.

Isaiah 11:2

"The Spirit of the Lord shall rest upon Him, The Spirit of wisdom and understanding, The Spirit of counsel and might, The Spirit of knowledge and of the fear of the Lord."

The Spiritual Reality:

The "Rest Upon Him" Clause: This implies a **Permanent Installation**. These spirits are not supposed to visit you; they are supposed to "Govern" from within you.

The Seven Fold Filter: This administrative team acts as a seven layer filter that sanitizes every influence trying to enter your "Gates."

The Verdict: You are telling the next generation: *"Do not try to be pure in your own strength! Invite the 'Seven Commissioners' to take over the administration of your vessel. When the Spirit of Might is on the job, the Marine Kingdom cannot find an entrance!"*

A Watchman's "Administrative Anointing" Decree

"I strike the Gavel and I authorize the 'Seven-Fold Spirit of the Lord' to take full administrative control over the Kingdom Estates of my children! I invoke Isaiah 11:2 and I decree that they are NOT relying on willpower, but on the Capacity of the Almighty!

"I activate the 'Intelligence Department'! I decree that the Spirit of Wisdom and Understanding is opening their eyes to see every trap and decode every 'Marine Fog'! They will not be deceived by the 'Normalization of Evil'!

"I commission the 'Enforcement Department'! I decree that the Spirit of Counsel and Might is resting upon them! When the pressure to compromise rises, they shall stand as 'Pillars of Zion' unshakable and firm!

"I establish the 'Compliance Department'! I decree that the Spirit of Knowledge and the Fear of the Lord is the atmosphere of their hearts! They will remember the Owner, they will guard the Seedbank, and they will manage the Estate with Absolute Integrity!

"We are raising 'High Capacity Governors'! They are clothed in the Seven Dimensions of the Spirit! The enemy is evicted, the Stewardship is Holy, and the King is Glorified! In Jesus' Name!"

The Governor's Verdict

A steward who is found unfaithful loses their "Administrative License" to walk in the fullness of Kingdom power. If you have neglected the Estate, you must file for Divine Receivership. You must hand the "deed" back to God and ask for a total restoration of the property.

The Executive Decree: "I renounce the lie that my body belongs to me. I recognize my office as a Steward of a Kingdom Estate. I repent for every unauthorized entry I allowed into this sanctuary. By the Gavel of the Just Judge, I evict every marine squatter and every illegal attachment from my body. I declare my Estate is under New Management, the management of Holiness and the Fear of the Lord, in the Name of Jesus!"

Chapter 2: The Cry of The Compromised

"I Wish I Had Listened": The Anatomy of Regret and the Mother's Warning

In the judicial corridors of the spirit, there is a sound that echoes louder than the crashing of waves: it is the **Cry of the Compromised**. This chapter moves from the structural analysis of the foundation to the emotional and spiritual "Crime Scene." We are examining the "Anatomy of Regret", the internal collapse that occurs when a soul realizes they have traded an eternal inheritance for a temporary sensation.

The Anatomy of Regret: The "Post Covenant" Collapse

Regret is not just a "feeling"; in the Kingdom, it is a **Judicial Indicator** that a spiritual robbery has taken place. It is the soul's alarm system signaling that an unauthorized transaction has been finalized.

The Sudden Nakedness: Just as Adam and Eve felt "naked" the moment they stepped outside of God's boundary, the "Illegal Merger" of sex before marriage triggers a loss of covering. The **"Garment of Glory"** that spiritual atmosphere of protection is stripped away. The soul suddenly feels exposed, cold, and vulnerable to the harsh elements of the deep. You went into the room seeking "connection," but you walked out feeling "discarded."

The Echo of the Conscience: Regret is the sound of the **Internal Gavel** striking against the heart. It is the heavy realization that you have signed a contract you cannot afford to pay, using the "Currency of Purity" that was meant to be the down payment on your marital throne. The conscience cries out because it knows a **Destiny Asset** has been misappropriated.

The "Weight of the Water": This specific form of regret often manifests as a heavy, "watery" depression a signature of the Marine

Kingdom. You feel like you are "underwater," struggling to breathe spiritually, because the weight of the compromise has submerged your joy. The "moisture" of the sin has turned into a flood that seeks to drown your confidence.

Proverbs 5:11-13
"And you mourn at last, when your flesh and your body are consumed, and say: 'How I have hated instruction, and my heart despised correction! I have not obeyed the voice of my teachers, nor inclined my ear to those who instructed me!'

The Spiritual Reality:
The "Mourn at Last" Clause: Regret is a delayed reaction. The enemy offers the "sweetness" at the beginning, but the "Mourning" is the final verdict. It is the "End of Contract" fee that the soul must pay.
The Despised Instruction: Notice that the cry of the compromised always points back to a **Warning** that was ignored. The "Mother's Warning" was the shield, but the rebellion was the hole in the armor.
The Verdict: You are telling the next generation: *"The 'I wish I had listened' cry is the most expensive sound in the world. Do not pay for a moment of pleasure with a lifetime of spiritual mourning. Listen to the Warning now, so you don't have to mourn at the last!"*

A Watchman's Decree Against the Spirit of Regret

"I strike the Gavel and I release the 'Spirit of Discernment' over my children! I invoke Proverbs 5:11 and I decree that they will **Not** be among those who 'mourn at the last'! I 'Veto' the spirit of rebellion that seeks to ignore the Mother's Warning!

"I command every 'Marine Fog' that creates the illusion of harmless pleasure to be **Scattered**! I decree that the 'Garment of

Glory' over my seed shall NOT be stripped! I 'Seal' the gates of their hearts against any transaction that would bankrupt their future!

"I speak to the 'Weight of the Water': I decree that my children will NOT be submerged in the depression of the deep! I command every 'Internal Gavel' of guilt to be silenced by the Blood of Repentance, and I decree a 'Quick Turning' back to the paths of Holiness!

"We are raising a generation that listens and lives! They will not trade their 'Throne Currency' for a gutter sensation! Their joy will remain above the water, and their foundation will remain dry! The warning is heard, the shield is up, and the Cry of the Compromised is **Silenced** in this bloodline! In Jesus' Name!"

The Mother's Warning: The Wisdom of the Watchman

The cry "I wish I had listened to my Mom" is a recurring theme in the dungeons of the deep. Why? Because the Mother is often the **First Line of Defense**, the primary "Watchman" over the generational foundation.

The Prophetic Alarm: A mother's warning is rarely about "rules"; it is about **Discernment**. Mothers often sense the "Marine Fog" on a partner long before the daughter or son sees it. They sense the "siphoning spirit" attached to the person trying to enter the bed of intimacy.

The Rejection of the Shield: When a young person rejects the mother's warning, they are not just "being independent"; they are **Decommissioning their Security System.** They are stepping outside the "Protective Perimeter" of the parental covenant, leaving themselves legally vulnerable to the "Predators of the Deep."

The Spirit of Rebellion: The "Salt" in the Wound

The "Cry of the Compromised" is fueled by the realization that **Disobedience** was the door opener.

The Legal Link: Rebellion against parental counsel and the Word of God acts as a "Legal Catalyst." It creates a chemical reaction in the spirit that "magnetizes" the individual to the Marine Kingdom.
The Rebellion Veil: Rebellion places a veil over the mind that makes the "Illegal Act" look like "True Love." It is only after the act is done, and the "Spirit of Disobedience" has finished its assignment, that the veil is lifted, and the soul is left standing in the ruins of their own integrity.

The "Hindsight" Prison

The Anatomy of Regret includes a mental prison where the individual constantly relives the moment of choice.
The Looping Tape: The enemy uses "Regret" as a **Monitoring Device.** He keeps playing the "Tape of Compromise" in your mind to keep you in a state of shame. Shame is the "handcuff" that keeps you from running to the Just Judge.
The Loss of Time: The greatest regret is not just the act itself, but the **Time Siphoned.** You realize that while you were chasing the "Illegal Merger," your real destiny was being warehoused. You cry because you realize you are "behind schedule" in the Kingdom.

The Turning Point: Converting Regret into Renunciation

In the judicial council of the home, we must teach our children that the "Cry of the Compromised" does not have to be a spiritual death sentence. While the enemy wants to use **Regret** to drown the soul in the "Weight of the Water," God uses Regret as a **Navigational Signal**. It is the internal compass indicating that you have drifted into enemy waters and must immediately execute a "U Turn."
To move from the "Crime Scene" to the "Restoration Room," the believer must learn the art of **Renunciation, Confession, Repentance and cleanse**, this is formal, legal rejection of the illegal merger.

The Judicial Shift: From Weeping to Warring

Regret is passive and heavy; Renunciation is active and fiery. The moment a soul realizes the foundation has been cracked, they must move from a posture of sorrow to a posture of **Legislative Authority**.

The Command of Fire: Instead of staying in the cycle of "I wish I had listened," the Governor learns to stand and say: *"I acknowledge the breach, but I now command the Fire of the Holy Ghost to consume the 'Soul Tie' and the 'Illegal Contract' I signed!"*

Stopping the Leak: Renunciation is the "Plugging of the Hole." It stops the siphoning of your marital honey and the seepage of the saltwater by revoking the enemy's "License to Dwell."

Mending the Shield: Re activating the Parental Altar

When a child engages in sex before marriage, they often discard the "Parental Shield" because of shame. Restoration requires a return to the **Structure of Authority**.

Returning to the Altar: True restoration involves a "Mending of the Shield." This happens when the child returns to the "Parental Altar," confesses the rebellion, and asks for the Mother or Father to re establish the spiritual "No Fly Zone" over their head.

Re activating the Shield: The Parental Warning was the original shield. By asking for forgiveness for the **rebellion** (not just the act), the child re aligns themselves with the "Generational Covering." This closes the gap that the spirit of harlotry used to enter the bloodline.

Joel 2:25

"So I will restore to you the years that the swarming locust has eaten, the crawling locust, the consuming locust, and the chewing locust..."

The Spiritual Reality:

The "Lust Locusts": Fornication sends "locusts" to eat the virtues and the "Genetic Trust" of your future. But God's promise is **Restoration** based on a return to His statutes.

The Judicial Restoration: God doesn't just "forget" the sin; He "Restores the Years." He can spiritually "re seal" a foundation that was cracked, provided there is a total renunciation of the old altar.
The Verdict: You are telling the next generation: *"Your mistake is not your identity! If you have compromised, do not stay in the 'Marine Fog.' Come back to the Altar, renounce the merger, and let the Judge of All the Earth restore your 'Garment of Glory'!"*

A Watchman's "Shield Restoration" Decree

"I strike the Gavel and I decree that the 'Cry of the Compromised' is being converted into the 'Shout of the Redeemed'! I invoke Joel 2:25 and I command a 'Supernatural Restoration' of every virtue eaten by the locusts of fornication!

"I authorize my children to move from Regret to Renunciation! I decree that they shall not drown in the 'Weight of the Water,' but they shall rise in the 'Power of the Fire'! I command every 'Illegal Contract' and 'Soul Tie' to be consumed now by the Fire of the Ghost!

"I re activate the 'Generational Shield' over my seed! I 'Veto' the spirit of shame that keeps children away from the Parental Altar! I decree a 'Mending of the Shield' and a 'Sealing of the Foundation'!

"We are a bloodline of the 'Second Chance'! What was cracked is being Mended; what was stolen is being Restored; and what was lost is being Found! We return to the Path of Holiness and we 'Lock the Gate' forever! In Jesus' Name!"

The Governor's Verdict

Regret is the "Saltwater" of the soul, but Repentance is the "Fire" that dries it up. If you are currently echoing the cry "I wish I had listened," realize that the Just Judge is still on the Throne. You cannot change the past, but you can **Sue for Restoration.**
The Executive Decree: "I silence the 'Cry of the Compromised' in my soul! I renounce the spirit of rebellion that made me deaf to the

warnings of my mother and the Word of God. I take the Gavel of Purity and I strike the 'Mirror of Regret.' I refuse to be a prisoner of my past mistakes. I bring my broken foundation to the Just Judge and I demand a total 'Repour' of my integrity! I am moving from the 'Dungeon of Shame' to the 'Throne of Grace,' in the Name of Jesus!"

The Spirit of Rebellion: Breaking the Link Between Disobedience and Disaster

In the judicial framework of the Kingdom, **Rebellion** is not just an attitude; it is a **Legal Catalyst**. The Scripture is blunt: *"For rebellion is as the sin of witchcraft, and stubbornness is as iniquity and idolatry"* (1Samuel:15:23). When an individual chooses to engage in sex before marriage, they are not just "following their heart", they are activating a spiritual law that links their disobedience directly to a future disaster.

The Witchcraft of Rebellion: Why does the Bible equate rebellion with witchcraft? Because both involve **The Transfer of Authority.**
The Illegal Handover: Witchcraft seeks to manipulate the spiritual realm through unauthorized power. Rebellion does the same; it takes the "Gavel of Decision" out of God's hand and places it in the hand of the "Self."
The Marine Signal: Rebellion sends a "Sonar Signal" into the Marine Kingdom. It announces to the deep: *"Here is a soul that has rejected the Government of Heaven."* This signal acts as an invitation for aquatic spirits to move in and provide "protection" and "comfort" that God's law now denies the rebel.

The "Disobedience to Disaster" Pipeline: In the natural world, a broken pipe leads to a flood. In the spiritual world, disobedience creates a **Pipeline of Disaster.**

The Structural Weakening: Every act of sexual disobedience "thins" the spiritual walls of your protection. You are effectively removing the "Fire Wall" of God's presence and replacing it with the "Saltwater" of compromise.
The Scheduled Disaster: The disaster linked to rebellion is often **Time Delayed.** The enemy allows you to enjoy the "pleasure of sin for a season" (Hebrews 11:25) while he quietly builds a "Gallows of Failure" in your future. This is why many experience a "Sudden Crash" in their finances, marriage, or health years after the secret rebellion began.

Breaking the Legal Link: The link between your disobedience and your disaster is a **Legal Chain.** It cannot be broken by "wishing it away"; it must be broken in the **Court of Heaven.**
The Admission of Guilt: You must stop calling it a "mistake" or a "lapse in judgment." You must call it **Rebellion.** Admission is the first step toward the "Writ of Severance."
The Blood Intervention: The only thing that can dissolve the "Legal Link" to disaster is the Blood of Jesus. The Blood speaks better things than the "Blood of the Sacrifice" made on the bed of fornication.
The Return to Authority: You must re establish the "Government of God" over your life. This means coming back under the authority of the Word, the Church, and parental counsel (where applicable).

Stubbornness as "Iniquity and Idolatry": In the spiritual administration of a Kingdom Estate, the most dangerous condition is not a single mistake, but the **"Hardening" of Rebellion**. This is what the Bible identifies as **Stubbornness**. It is a state where the Steward refuses to acknowledge the "Indicators of Decay" and continues to operate the Estate in direct violation of the Manufacturer's Manual.

The Idolatry of Self: The Altar of "I Feel"

In the judicial framework, idolatry is the act of giving a "Foreign Authority" the seat of final judgment in your life.

The Feelings Idol: When a believer says, *"I know what the Bible says, but I feel..."*, they have performed an act of **Legislative Idolatry**. They have removed the Word of God from the bench and seated their own "Feelings" as the Supreme Judge.

Worshiping Desires: By prioritizing a temporary sensation over a Divine Statute, you are effectively worshiping your own desires on the altar of your body. You are telling the Creator: *"My appetite is more sovereign than Your Law."*

The Marine Hardening: Caging the Heart

The Marine Kingdom is a master of **"Atmospheric Hardening."** They understand that as long as a heart is "soft" (repentant), they cannot maintain a legal foothold.

The Shell of Stubbornness: The enemy works to "Cage the Heart" in a thick shell of stubbornness. This shell acts as a **Frequency Jammer**, making you "Hard Hearted" toward the warnings of God, the advice of parents, and the prick of your conscience.

The "Soft Heart" Deception: Paradoxically, while the heart becomes hard toward God, it becomes dangerously **"Soft Hearted"** toward the very people who are siphoning your destiny. The enemy makes you "compassionate" toward your predator and "defensive" against your protector. This is a spiritual "Stockholm Syndrome" designed to keep the siphons attached until the Estate is empty.

1 Samuel 15:23

"For rebellion is as the sin of witchcraft, and stubbornness is as iniquity and idolatry."

The Spiritual Reality:

The "Witchcraft" Connection: Rebellion is compared to witchcraft because both seek to bypass God's authority to get a desired result.

The "Iniquity and Idolatry" Verdict: Stubbornness is not a "personality trait"; it is a **Judicial Crime**. It is the active refusal to submit the Estate to its rightful Owner.

The Verdict: You are telling the next generation: *"Stubbornness is the 'Concrete' that seals your mistakes into your foundation. If you remain stubborn, you are not just 'sinning' you are worshiping a false god called 'Self.' Break the shell before the shell breaks you!"*

A Watchman's "Heart Softening" Decree

"I strike the Gavel and I shatter the 'Shell of Stubbornness' over my children! I invoke 1 Samuel 15:23 and I decree that the 'Idolatry of Self' is **Broken** in our bloodline! I 'Veto' the lie that feelings are more sovereign than the Word of the Living God!

"I command the 'Marine Hardening' to melt away by the Fire of the Holy Ghost! I decree that my seed shall be 'Soft Hearted' toward the Voice of the Lord and 'Hard Hearted' against the whispers of the destiny thief! I 'Uncage' their hearts from the spirit of rebellion!

"I decree a 'Resurrection of Submission' in our home! I command the 'Frequency Jammers' to cease and desist! My children will hear the Warning, they will heed the Correction, and they will Honor the Owner of the Estate!

"We are raising a generation of 'Soft Soil'! They will be easily entreated by Wisdom and fiercely resistant to Folly! The idols are toppled, the shell is broken, and the heart is FREE! In Jesus' Name!"

The "Disaster Prevention" Protocol: As a **Governor of Light**, your job is to intercept the disaster before it manifests.

Repentance as an Interceptor: Strategic repentance "Blows up the Pipeline." It cuts off the flow of judgment before it reaches the "City of your Future."
The Seven Fold Restitution: According to the Law, when a thief (the spirit of rebellion) is caught, he must restore seven fold (Proverbs 6:31). You must demand that every virtue siphoned through your rebellion be returned to your foundation.

The Governor's Verdict: Disobedience is a "Contract for Disaster," but the **Just Judge** is willing to tear up the contract if the rebel will become a **Steward.** You must break the link today or the disaster will claim your tomorrow.

The Executive Decree:
"In the Name of Jesus, I identify the Spirit of Rebellion that has operated in my foundation! I renounce every act of disobedience and every moment I rejected the counsel of the Word and the watchmen in my life. I take the 'Sword of the Spirit' and I **Sever** the link between my past disobedience and my future disaster! I decree that the 'Pipeline of Decay' is shattered by the Fire of God. I return to the Government of Heaven. I am no longer a rebel; I am a Governor of Integrity! The disaster is canceled, and my restoration is established, **In The Name Of Jesus!"**

Chapter 3: The Illiteracy of The Soul

"This Book of the Law": Why Ignorance of Scripture Leads to the Bed of Fornication (Joshua: 1:8)

In the spiritual administration of a Governor, **Illiteracy is a Security Breach.** When God commanded Joshua at the threshold of the Promised Land, He didn't give him a sword first; He gave him a **Legal Mandate**: *"This Book of the Law shall not depart from your mouth, but you shall meditate in it day and night, that you may observe to do according to all that is written in it"* (Joshua 1:8). The "Bed of Fornication" is almost always prepared in the "Room of Ignorance." If your soul is illiterate to the Laws of the Kingdom, you will unknowingly sign away your inheritance to the Marine Kingdom.

The "Scriptural Shield" and the Anatomy of the Fall

Ignorance of the Word is not a passive state; it is a **Vulnerability**.

The Absent Filter: When the Word of God is not "meditated on day and night," the mind lacks the judicial filter required to process "Romantic Suggestion." Without the Law, a "Lustful Impulse" is misidentified as "True Love."

The Marine Strategy: The Marine Kingdom thrives in the dark. They count on the fact that you haven't read the "Terms and Conditions" of your own soul. If you don't know that your body is a **Kingdom Estate**, you will treat it like a "Common Rental," allowing any passing spirit to occupy it for a night.

Meditate Day and Night": The Internal Gavel

The command to meditate is a command to **Internalize the Judiciary.**

The Living Word: Meditation turns the Word from "ink on paper" into a "Living Gavel" inside your heart. When temptation arrives, the Word should "speak" before your hormones do.

The Failure of Literacy: If you "allow" yourself to fornicate, it is a direct indicator that you have not read, or have not submitted to, the Law. You cannot be "Born Again" and "Biblically Literate" while simultaneously participating in the "Mother of Harlotry." To do so is to have a **Divided Ledger**, which the Just Judge will not validate.

The Blind Leading the Blind: The Covenant of Ignorance

When two people decide to engage in sex before marriage, they are forming a **Covenant of Illiteracy.**

The Mutual Blind Spot: If the person you are with is pushing you to fornicate, it is the ultimate proof that they do not have the **Fear of the Lord**. They have not read the Book. They are not stewards; they are "Destiny Raiders."

The Legal Trap: By joining yourself to someone who ignores the Law, you are tethering your foundation to a "Legal Outlaw." You are entering a merger where neither party knows the "Tax Penalties" (spiritual consequences) of the transaction.

Observing to Do": The Bridge to Prosperity

Joshua 1:8 links "observing to do" with "making your way prosperous."

The Inverse Law: If you do *not* observe the Law regarding your body, the inverse becomes true: you make your way **Precarious**.

The Illiteracy Tax: Every act of fornication is a "tax" paid to the Marine Kingdom. Because you didn't know the Law protected your virtue, you paid the enemy with the currency of your future peace. Spiritual illiteracy is the most expensive condition on earth.

Reclaiming the Governor's Library

To stop the decay, you must return to the **Book of the Law.**

The Search of Title: You must go back to the Word to find out who you really are. You are not a "Sexual Being" first; you are a **Royal Priest**.

De programming the Marine Culture: The culture (movies, music, social media) has "educated" your soul in the ways of the deep. You must use the Word of God as a "Spiritual Detergent" to wash the "Liquid Sorcery" out of your mind.

The Governor's Verdict: Ignorance is not an excuse in the Court of Heaven; it is a **Forfeiture of Rights.** If you have ended up in the bed of fornication, it is because you dropped your Shield of the Word. You must pick up the Book, eat the Scroll, and let the Law of God become the "Boundary Line" of your intimacy.

The Executive Decree:

"I renounce the 'Illiteracy of the Soul'! I repent for every time I ignored 'The Book of the Law' to follow the impulses of my flesh. I declare that from this day, the Word of God shall not depart from my mouth! I will meditate on Holiness day and night. I strike the Gavel against the spirit of ignorance that led me into illegal mergers. I am a Biblically Literate Governor, and I refuse to be tricked by the 'Mother of Harlotry' ever again! My foundation is built on the Rock of the Word, In The name of Jesus!"

The Fear of The Lord: The Missing Component in Modern Relationships

In the administrative cabinet of a Governor, the **Fear of the Lord** is not an "emotion" of terror; it is the **Foundational Regulator**. Scripture defines it as the *"beginning of wisdom"* (Psalm111:10) and the *"fountain of life, to turn one away from the snares of death"* (Proverbs 14:27). In modern relationships, the absence of this fear has created a "Lawless Zone" where individuals believe they can negotiate with God's standards without facing the judicial consequences of the Deep.

The Fear of the Lord as a Spiritual Boundary: The Fear of the Lord acts as the **Sovereign Fence** around your Kingdom Estate.
The Invisible Witness: When two people have no fear of the Lord, they act as if they are in a vacuum, believing that "if no one sees us, it doesn't count." However, the Governor knows that the Just Judge is the third party in every room.
The Regulatory Failure: Without the Fear of the Lord, "Consent" becomes the only standard for intimacy. But in the Kingdom, **Covenant** not just consent is the requirement. Engaging in sex because "both parties want to" while ignoring God's "No" is a direct act of treason against the King's Government.

The "Modern Relationship" Delusion: Modern culture has replaced the Fear of the Lord with "Relatability" and "Vibes."
The Absence of Awe: When you lose the awe of God's holiness, you lose the ability to see sin as **Toxic**. You begin to see fornication as a "small compromise" rather than a "Structural Breach."
The Partner Audit: If the person seeking intimacy with you has no fear of the Lord, they are fundamentally **Untrustworthy**. A person who will cheat on God to be with you will eventually cheat on you to be with someone else. Their foundation is built on the shifting sands of desire, not the bedrock of Divine Accountability.

The "Snares of Death" and the Marine Connection: Proverbs14:27 tells us that the Fear of the Lord turns us away from the *"snares of death."* **The Marine Trap:** The Marine Kingdom sets "Sexual Snares" that look like "Romantic Opportunities." Without the Fear of the Lord, you lack the **Judicial Discernment** to see the hook inside the bait.

The Preservation of Virtue: The Fear of the Lord acts as a "Spiritual Repellent" against aquatic spirits. When you carry the weight of God's presence (Kavod), you become "Heavy" in the spirit. You are no longer "Light Cargo" that can be easily swept away into the marine vaults of harlotry.

In the spiritual geography of the Kingdom, the "Dry Ground" of holiness is surrounded by the treacherous waters of the Marine Kingdom. Without the proper navigation tools, a Steward will mistake a **Sinking Trap** for a **Saving Harbor**. This section explores the "Snares of Death" high level spiritual entanglements designed to pull a destiny from the heights of Zion into the vaults of the abyss.

The Marine Trap: The "Hook inside the Bait"

The Marine Kingdom is a realm of **Illusion**. It rarely presents itself as "evil"; instead, it presents itself as "desirable."

Romantic Opportunities vs. Sexual Snares: The enemy sets snares that look like "True Love" or "Once in a Lifetime Romance." These are specifically designed to bypass your logic and target your emotions.

The Lack of Judicial Discernment: Without the **Fear of the Lord**, the soul is spiritually "blind." You see the "Bait" (the attention, the physical attraction, the promises) but you lack the capacity to see the "Hook" (the soul tie, the destiny siphon, and the ancestral debt). The Fear of the Lord is the "X-Ray Vision" that reveals the metal hook hidden inside the sweet bait.

The Preservation of Virtue: The Power of Being "Heavy"

In the spirit, holiness has **Mass**. Sin, however, makes a person "Light" and easily movable.

The Spiritual Repellent: The Fear of the Lord acts as a "Frequency Repellent" against aquatic spirits. Just as certain oils repel insects, the atmosphere of **Kavod** (the Weighty Glory of God) makes your vessel repulsive to marine entities. They cannot "grip" a soul that is saturated in the Fear of the Lord.

The Heavy Cargo Protocol: When you carry the weight of God's presence, you become **"Heavy"** in the spirit. In the physical world, it is hard for a current to sweep away a heavy anchor. In the spirit, a person who fears God is "Heavy Cargo." You cannot be easily swept away by the "Tides of Trend" or the "Currents of Lust." You are anchored to the Rock, and the marine vaults of harlotry have no power to pull you under.

Proverbs 14:27

The fear of the Lord is a fountain of life, to turn one away from the snares of death."

The Spiritual Reality: The "Fountain of Life": Notice that the Fear of the Lord is a "Fountain." It is a constant upward flow of life that pushes *against* the downward pull of the "Snares of Death."

The "Turning" Mechanism: This is a **Judicial Pivot**. The Fear of the Lord doesn't just show you the snare; it provides the **Force** to "Turn you away." It is your spiritual power steering.

The Verdict: You are telling the next generation: *"The ocean of this world is full of hooks. If you walk without the Fear of the Lord, you are 'Light Cargo' waiting to be stolen. But if you carry the Weight of the King, you become 'Un swappable' and 'Un stoppable'! Keep your Kavod heavy and your eyes open!"*

A Watchman's "Snare-Breaker" Decree:

"I strike the Gavel and I decree a 'Supernatural Heaviness' over the souls of my children! I invoke Proverbs 14:27 and I declare that the Fear of the Lord is a 'Fountain of Life' in our bloodline, pushing back every 'Snare of Death'!

"I 'Veto' every romantic trap and sexual snare disguised as an opportunity! I decree that my seed shall not be 'Light Cargo' for the marine kingdom! I command the **Kavod** the Weighty Glory of God to rest upon their bodies and spirits, making them 'Too Heavy' for the enemy to carry!

"I activate 'Judicial Discernment' in their minds! I decree that they shall see the 'Hook inside the Bait' with 20/20 clarity! I command the 'Marine Repellent' of the Holy Ghost to saturate their atmosphere, making them untouchable to aquatic spirits!

"We are anchored to the Rock! We are turning away from the snares and walking toward the Throne! The 'Snares of Death' are broken, the 'Fountain of Life' is flowing, and our seed is SAFE! In Jesus' Name!"

The "No Compromise" Standard

In the spiritual administration of your life, holiness and righteousness are not optional "upgrades" or lifestyle suggestions; they are the **Non Negotiable Qualities** of a true believer. To be a Governor of the Dry Ground, you must move beyond the "struggle" mentality and adopt a **Legislative Standard** that refuses to bend to the pressures of the deep.

The Integrity of the Governor: Holiness as Primary Policy

In the natural world, a government operates based on its "Primary Policy." If the policy is "Security," every decision is filtered through that lens.

Beyond "Trying": A Governor does not simply "try" to be holy; they govern their body with the **Fear of the Lord** as their Primary Policy. This means holiness is the "Default Setting" of the Estate.

The Executive Decision: When the policy of holiness is firmly established, you no longer have to debate with temptation. The decision was already made in the "Judicial Chambers" of your heart long before the opportunity for compromise ever appeared.

Breaking the "Normalcy" Bias: Shattering the Routine

We live in a culture and unfortunately, many modern churches that has normalized sexual "falling" as a routine, expected part of dating. This is the **"Normalcy Bias,"** a deceptive atmosphere that makes the "Normalization of Evil" look like "Grace."

The Auction Block: Without the Fear of the Lord, your body becomes an item for sale on the "Auction Block" of affection. You trade your purity to whoever offers the most attention, the most "likes," or the most emotional comfort.

The Sacred Trust: The Fear of the Lord shatters this normalcy. It demands that we treat our bodies as **Sacred Trusts**. A Sacred Trust cannot be auctioned; it is reserved exclusively for the purpose and person designated by the Owner. You are telling the world: *"I am not for sale. I have been pre sold to the King, and my body is a Restricted Zone!"*

1 Peter 1:15-16

"But as He who called you is holy, you also be holy in all your conduct, because it is written, 'Be holy, for I am holy.'

The Spiritual Reality: The "As He Is" Standard: The metric for your holiness is not "what other people are doing" or "what the modern church allows." The metric is the **Nature of God Himself**.

The "In All Your Conduct" Clause: This is a **Total Jurisdiction** mandate. It covers your private messages, your late night conversations, and your dating life. There is no "Grey Area" in a Kingdom Estate.

The Verdict: You are telling the next generation: *"Do not follow the 'Normal' path, for the 'Normal' path leads to a cracked foundation.*

Be an 'Exceptional Governor'! Set a standard that makes the world wonder why you are so firm. Holiness is your Power, not your Burden!"

A Watchman's "no Compromise" Decree:

I strike the Gavel and I establish the 'Standard of Zion' over the households of our bloodline! I invoke 1 Peter 1:15 and I decree that my children shall be 'Holy in **All** their conduct'! I 'Veto' the normalcy bias of this generation!

"I decree that our bodies are **Not** on the auction block! I cancel every 'Sale of Affection' and I 'Withdraw' every bid from the kingdom of darkness! We are **Reserved** for the King! I decree that Holiness is our 'Primary Policy' and Righteousness is our 'National Identity'!

"I command every 'Grey Area' in our minds to be illuminated by the Fire of Truth! We refuse to normalize the 'Falling'! We choose to normalize the 'Standing'! I decree that my children are 'Structural Masterpieces' of Integrity, built on a foundation that does not bend!

"We are the Governors of the Dry Ground! We do not compromise with the moisture of the deep! Our standard is set, our conduct is Holy, and our King is Glorified! In Jesus' Name!"

Re-establishing the Gavel of Awe: To restore the Fear of the Lord in your relationships, you must perform a **System Reset.**

The Judicial Recall: You must recall every area where you treated God's Word as a "suggestion" rather than a "Statute."

The Seven Dimensions of Power: It is the *Spirit of the Fear of the Lord* (Isaiah 11:2) that gives you the administrative power to say "No" when your flesh says "Yes." It provides the "Might" to maintain your consecration in a defiled generation.

The Governor's Verdict

A relationship without the Fear of the Lord is a building without a permit; it is illegal and destined for the wrecking ball of the Deep. If you find yourself in a union where God is not feared, you are in a **Disaster Zone**. You must repent for devaluing the King and re institute the Fear of the Lord as the Chief Justice of your heart.

The Executive Decree:

I repent for the casual way I have treated the Holiness of God! I renounce every relationship and every 'Vibe' that was built on the absence of the Fear of the Lord. I receive the Spirit of Awe and Reverence into my soul today. I strike the Gavel against the 'Spirit of the Age' that seeks to normalize compromise. I declare that my body and my future marriage are governed by the Fear of the Almighty! I am a Governor who trembles at the Word, and I will not trade my Birthright for the soup of disobedience, **In The Name Of Jesus!"**

Part II: The Mechanics of Invisible Covenants

Chapter 4: The Illegal Merger

Forming Covenants with Demons: The Spiritual Exchange During Fornication

In the administrative courts of the spirit, sex is never "just sex." It is a **Judicial Act of Union.** When two people join together outside the legal framework of marriage, they are performing an **Illegal Merger**, a spiritual transaction that bypasses the protection of God and invites third party entities to the table. This is the moment where "Two become One," but in the bed of fornication, that "One" becomes a gateway for a host of demonic squatters.

The Law of the "One Flesh" Merger (1Corinthians 6:15-18)

The Apostle Paul, acting as a Kingdom Prosecutor, lays out the legal reality: *"Do you not know that your bodies are members of Christ? Shall I then take the members of Christ and make them members of a harlot? Certainly not! Or do you not know that he who is joined to a harlot is one body with her?"*

The Spiritual Glue: The word "joined" it means to be "glued" or "cemented" together. This is not a temporary physical touch; it is a permanent **Covenant Seal.**

The Illegal Transfer: When you join your body (which is a member of Christ) to someone carrying demonic "cargo," you are creating a bridge for that cargo to enter your estate. If they have a spirit of suicide, depression, or a marine spirit spouse, that entity now has a **Legal Right** to walk across the bridge of your intimacy and occupy your foundation.

The Altar of the Bed: Sacrifice and Exchange: Every sexual act is an act of **Priesthood.** You are officiating at an altar. In marriage, the altar is holy. In fornication, the altar is "Profane."

The Blood and Fluid Covenant: In the spirit, sexual fluids carry the "Life Force" of the individual (Leviticus 17:11 *"the life of the flesh is in the blood"*). When these are exchanged in an illegal union, it is viewed by the Dark Kingdom as a **Sacrifice.**

The Demonic Signature: Demonic entities, specifically those from the Marine Kingdom, watch for these "Sacrifices." They use the fluids of the fornicator as "ink" to sign a **Demonic Covenant.** You think you are just "spending the night," but the enemy is recording a "Permanent Occupancy Agreement" in the Ledger of the Deep.

The "Mother of Harlots" and the Global Syndicate (Revelation 17:1-5)

The Bible speaks of a mystery: *"Babylon the Great, the mother of Harlots and of the Abominations of the Earth."* **The Infrastructure of Lust:** This is the spiritual "Headquarters" of all sexual corruption. When you fornicate, you are not just "sinning against yourself"; you are **Trading with the Mother of Harlots.**

The Siphoning Effect: She uses sex to "Drunk the inhabitants of the earth with the wine of her fornication." This "wine" is a spiritual sedative that makes you forget your destiny. While you are intoxicated by the pleasure, her "Trade Agents" are in your soul, siphoning out your virtue, your prophetic dreams, divine destiny and your financial "honey."

The Collection of Spirits: The "Crowded Bed"

When you enter into an illegal merger, you are not just sleeping with one person; you are sleeping with **everyone they have ever slept with.**

The Chain of Attachment: If Person A sleeps with Person B, and Person B has slept with 10 others, Person A is now spiritually "merged" with the entire chain. This is why many people feel "crowded" in their minds or have "competing voices" in their heads after a life of fornication.

The Rattle of the Spirits: As a **Governor**, you must understand that these spirits become "rattled" when you try to enter a real, godly marriage later. They appear in your dreams as "Previous Lovers" because they still have a **Legal Attachment** to your foundation. They are squatters fighting against your new, holy union.

Breaking the Invisible Bond (Matthew 18:18)

"Whatever you bind on earth will be bound in heaven, and whatever you loose on earth will be loosed in heaven."

The Writ of Severance: Because the merger was **Illegal** (unlicensed by God), you have the right to sue for a **Divorce Decree** in the Court of Heaven.

The Judicial Renunciation: You must specifically name the "mergers," renounce the "merger fluids," and command the "merger spirits" to vacate the Kingdom Estate.

The Governor's Verdict: An illegal merger is a "hostile takeover" of your soul. You cannot simply "move on" from a past lover; you must **Legally Dismantle the Union.** If you do not, you are bringing a "third party" into your future marriage bed, and that spirit will be the one that causes the "unexplained" chaos in your home.

The Executive Decree:

"I stand in the Court of Heaven as a Governor of Light! I identify every 'Illegal Merger' I have ever formed through the bed of fornication. I bring the Blood of Jesus over the 'Covenant Fluids' and the 'Soul Ties' created in those unions. By the Gavel of the Just Judge, I declare these mergers **Null and Void!** I issue a Writ of Severance against every demon, every marine entity, and every 'Mother of Harlots' agent attached to my intimacy. I am de registered from the

Ledger of the Deep! My body is a Holy Estate, and I declare it 'Single and Consecrated' for the King, **In The Name of Jesus!"**

The Mother of Harlots: Identifying the Global Source of Sexual Abominations (Revelation 17:5)

In the spiritual geography of the dark kingdom, there is a central "Headquarters" for all sexual corruption. The Apostle John, in his judicial vision, identifies this entity: *"And on her forehead a name was written* ***Mystery, Babylon the Great, The Mother of Harlots And Of The Abominations Of The Earth****."* To understand sex before marriage, a Governor must look past the physical act and identify the **Global Source** that fuels it.

The Mystery of the "Mother" System: In the judicial mapping of spiritual conflict, we must identify the source of the "Marine Fog" and the "Spirit of Harlotry." The Scripture identifies a high level architect of systemic decay: the **"Mother of Harlots."** The title "Mother" signifies that this entity is a **Life Giver to Evil**. She is the spiritual "Womb" those births and sustains every form of sexual perversion, from fornication and adultery to the institutionalization of abominations.

The Reproductive Nature of Sin: Adopting a Nature

When we discuss the "Mother" system, we are discussing **Lineage**. Every child is influenced by the nature of their parent.

Parented by the System: When a young person engages in fornication, they are doing more than committing a solo act; they are being **"Parented"** by this system. By participating in her "Sexual Philosophy," they are effectively adopting her nature. They begin to speak her language, value her "temporary sensations," and ignore the "Manufacturer's Manual."

The Exchange of Identity: Fornication is an invitation for this "Mother" to imprint her character onto your foundation. You go in as a Child of the Kingdom, but you emerge carrying the spiritual "DNA" of a harlot system.

The Global Reach: The Streaming of Decay

Revelation 17:1 describes this entity as sitting on **"many waters."** In the judicial interpretation of prophecy, "waters" represent peoples, multitudes, nations, and tongues.

The Global Standard: This means her influence is not localized; it is a **Global Stream**. Her "Sexual Philosophy" is streamed through global media, music, fashion, and social algorithms. She is the one responsible for making the "Normalization of Evil" a worldwide standard.

The Media Altar: Every time a child consumes media that glamorizes sex before marriage, they are sitting at the "Table of the Mother" She uses entertainment to "Dampen" the conscience and prepare the soil of the heart for the "Wet Ground" of compromise.

Revelation 17:1–2

"Come, I will show you the judgment of the great harlot who sits on many waters, with whom the kings of the earth committed fornication, and the inhabitants of the earth were made drunk with the wine of her fornication."

The Spiritual Reality:

The "Made Drunk" Clause: Compromise begins with **Intoxication**. The "Wine of Fornication" is the cultural narrative that makes sin look "fun," "harmless," or "modern." When a soul is "drunk" on this wine, they lose their spiritual balance and judicial discernment.

The Judgment Mandate: The Angel tells John, "I will show you the **judgment**." As Governors, we do not fear this system; we enforce the judgment already written against it.
The Verdict: You are telling the next generation: *"You are being targeted by a global 'Streaming Service' of decay! The 'Mother of Harlots' wants to parent your desires and intoxicate your judgment. Do not drink her wine! Stay sober in the Word so you can recognize the system for what it is a doomed entity under the Judgment of God!"*

A watchman's "Systemic Separation" Decree

"I strike the Gavel and I decree a 'Spiritual Divorce' between my seed and the 'Mother of Harlots' system! I invoke Revelation 17 and I declare that the 'Wine of Fornication' shall NOT intoxicate the hearts of my children!

"I 'Veto' every attempt of this system to 'Parent' the desires of my household! I decree that our children are Parented by the Spirit of Truth and Nourished by the Bread of Life! I command every 'Global Stream' of perversion in their media and environment to be **Blocked** by the Fire of the Holy Ghost!

"I decree that my seed shall not sit on the 'Many Waters' of compromise! We are 'Dry Ground' believers! I command the 'DNA of Harlotry' to be purged from our bloodline and replaced with the 'DNA of Holiness'!

"We refuse the global standard! We set the Kingdom Standard! I decree that the 'Fog' of this system is lifted and the 'Light of Zion' is manifest! Our children are Sober, our children are Pure, and the Mother of Harlots has **No Part** in our Estate! In Jesus' Name!"

The Wine of Fornication: The Spiritual Sedative

"...with whom the kings of the earth committed fornication, and the inhabitants of the earth were made drunk with the wine of her fornication" (Revelation 17:2).

The Loss of Judicial Clarity: Just as a drunk man cannot drive a car or make a legal decision, a soul "drunk" on the wine of the Mother of Harlots cannot see the disaster ahead. This "wine" is the dopamine hit of secret lust and the cultural validation of "hookup culture."

The Siphoning Effect: While you are "intoxicated" by the pleasure, the agents of the Mother are performing a **Resource Extraction.** They are siphoning the "Gold" of your purpose and the "Silver" of your peace, replacing it with the "Dross" of shame and the "Lead" of depression.

The Marine Registry and the "Beast" Connection

The Mother of Harlots is seen riding a "Scarlet Beast." This Beast represents the **Executive Power** of the dark kingdom, often surfacing from the Sea (Revelation 13:1).

The Marine Altar: This entity is the Chief Administrator of the **Marine Trading Floors.** When you engage in sex before marriage, your name is entered into her "Registry of Harlotry."

The Branding: Revelation 17:5 says the name was on her *forehead.* This is about **Mindset.** She seeks to brand the minds of this generation so they can no longer distinguish between "Love" and "Lust," or "Covenant" and "Contract."

The "Abominations" and the Defilement of the Land

The Scripture calls her the Mother of **Abominations.** An abomination is something that causes "Spiritual Nausea" to the Almighty.

The Entry Point: Sex before marriage is the "Gateway Abomination." Once the mother of Harlots gets you to compromise your bed, she has the legal right to introduce more "Abominations" into your life, abortion, gender confusion, and suicidal ideation.

The Anger of the Lord: This global system is designed specifically to provoke the Lord to anger, thereby removing the "Fire Wall" of His protection from a nation or a family bloodline.

The Verdict of the Just Judge: "Come Out of Her"

In **Revelation18:4**, a voice from heaven cries: *"Come out of her, my people, lest you share in her sins, and lest you receive of her plagues."*

The Executive Withdrawal: You cannot "fix" the Mother of Harlots; you must **Withdraw your Citizenship** from her kingdom. This requires a judicial renunciation of her "Wine" and her "Standard."

Breaking the Parental Link: You must declare that you are no longer a "Child of Harlotry" but a "Child of the Light." You must cut the "Spiritual Umbilical Cord" that connects your sexuality to the Babylonian system.

The Governor's Verdict

The Mother of Harlots is a "Destiny Assassin" who uses the bed of fornication as her hunting ground. As a Governor, you must recognize that your struggle with lust is not just "human nature", it is a **Global Syndicate** trying to annex your territory. You must use the Gavel to strike the Mother of Harlots out of your foundation.

The Executive Decree:

"I stand in the Light of the Word and I identify the Mother of Harlots! I renounce her 'Wine' and her 'Abominations.' I declare that I am no longer intoxicated by the seductions of the deep. By the Gavel of the Just Judge, I SEVER every link between my body and the Babylonian system of harlotry! I de register my name from the Marine Registry of Lust. I come out of her and I consecrate my vessel for the King of Glory alone. My sexuality is governed by Zion, not Babylon, **In The name of Jesus**!"

Chapter 5: The Marine Connection

The Liquid Grave: How the Marine Kingdom Siphons Destiny via Sexual Altars

In the spiritual geography of the dark kingdom, the sea is not just a body of water; it is a **Judicial Territory** and a warehouse for stolen human capital. As a Governor, you must understand that the Marine Kingdom (the "Deep") is the primary beneficiary of the sin of fornication. When an individual engages in sex before marriage, they are not just "committing a sin"; they are performing a **Sacrifice on a Sexual Altar** that siphons their destiny into what the Bible calls the "Liquid Grave."

The Sea as a Cemetery of Destinies (Ezekiel 27:34)

The Prophet Ezekiel gives us a chilling judicial observation: *"In the time when you are broken by the seas in the depths of the waters, your merchandise and the entire company in your midst will fall."*

The Sinking of the "Ship of Destiny": Every human life is a "Merchant Ship" carrying a cargo of purpose, marriage, wealth, and prophetic calling.

The Marine Strike: Fornication act as a "Torpedo" that strikes the hull of your ship. The moment the act is committed, the structural integrity of your life is breached, and the "merchandise" (your future) begins to sink into the marine vaults.

The Liquid Grave: This is why many people, after a life of sexual compromise, feel "empty." It is because their "company" their joy, their focus, and their spiritual weight, has fallen to the bottom of the sea.

The Sexual Altar: The Pumping Station of the Deep: In the spirit realm, the bed of fornication is a **Trading Floor.**

The Transaction: You give the "Liquid Pleasure" of the moment, and the Marine Kingdom takes the "Liquid Virtue" of your future.

The Siphoning Mechanism: Just as a pump moves water from one place to another, the sexual act outside of marriage acts as a "Siphon." It pumps the "Honey" of your future marriage and the "Oil" of your anointing directly into the marine treasuries.

The Marine Spirits (Job 41:1): Leviathan and other aquatic princes preside over these siphoning stations. They "play" with the fornicator, leading them into deeper "waters" of perversion until the individual is completely submerged in the "Liquid Grave" of addiction and shame.

The "Cargo" at the Bottom of the Sea (Revelation 18:11-13)

"The merchants of the earth will weep and mourn over her because no one buys their cargoes anymore. **12** cargoes of gold, silver, precious stones and pearls; fine linen, purple, silk and scarlet cloth; every sort of citron wood, and articles of every kind made of ivory, costly wood, bronze, iron and marble. **13** cargoes of cinnamon and spice, of incense, myrrh and frankincense; of wine and olive oil, of fine flour and wheat; cattle and sheep; horses and carriages; **and human beings sold as slaves.**

The Soul Vaults: At the bottom of the spiritual sea, there are "Warehouses" containing the stolen cargo of fornicators. Your ability to have a stable marriage, your financial "River of Life," and your peace of mind are often locked in these underwater vaults.

The Mystery of the Missing Destiny: This is why you may pray for success but never see it. The "Cargo" of your destiny is sitting at the bottom of the sea because of a foundational sexual altar that was never dismantled.

The "Liquid Sorcery" of Marine Intimacy: Sex before marriage is often fueled by a specific type of **Marine Sorcery** (Pharmakia).
The Intoxication: Aquatic spirits release a "Spiritual Pheromone" that makes the wrong person look like the "One." It creates an artificial "chemistry" that is actually a **Spiritual Sedative.**
The Drowning of the Conscience: While you are "drowning" in the sensations of the flesh, you are actually being pulled under the "Surface of Sanity." This is why fornicators often make decisions that "sink" their reputation and their future, they are operating from the bottom of the Liquid Grave.

The Judicial Retrieval (Amos 9:3)

The Lord God gives an executive order to His agents: *"And though they hide themselves on top of Carmel, from there I will search and take them; and though they hide from My sight at the bottom of the sea, from there I will command the serpent, and it shall bite them."*
No Hiding Place: Even if your destiny has been "sunk" to the bottom of the sea, the **Just Judge** has the authority to retrieve it.
The Repossession Order: As a Governor, you don't just "ask" for your destiny back; you issue a **Repossession Order.** You command the Marine Kingdom to vomit up your cargo.

The Governor's Verdict

Fornication is the "Anchor" that drags your destiny into the Liquid Grave. If you feel like your life is "underwater," it is time to cut the chain. You must de register from the marine sexual altars and sue for the retrieval of your sunken cargo.

The Executive Decree:

"I stand as a Governor of the Dry Ground and I identify the 'Liquid Grave' where my destiny was sunk! I strike the Gavel against every marine altar of fornication! I command the Marine Kingdom: **Vomit**

Up My Cargo! I repossess my marriage, my finances, and my spiritual clarity from the underwater vaults. I declare that the siphoning is over! By the Blood of Jesus, I cut every anchor of shame and I rise to the surface of my purpose. My destiny is no longer at the bottom of the sea; it is seated in the Heights with Christ, **In The Name Of Jesus!"**

The Cargo at The Bottom of The Sea: Locating Your Hijacked Future (Ezekiel 27:34)

In the judicial archives of the spirit, every child of God is seen as a "Merchant Ship" destined to deliver a specific cargo to the shores of their generation. This cargo includes your **marital peace, financial abundance, prophetic sharp sightedness, and the "oil" of your anointing.** However, when you engage in sex before marriage, you provide the Marine Kingdom with the "Legal Coordinates" to hijack your ship. As a Governor, you must understand that your current "lack" is not a lack of provision, but a case of **Hijacked Assets.**

The Anatomy of the Hijack

The Marine Kingdom operates like spiritual pirates. They do not create wealth or virtue; they **harvest** it from the disobedient.

The Vulnerability: Ezekiel 27:34 states, *"In the time when you are broken by the seas in the depths of the waters, your merchandise... will fall."* Fornication is the "Breach" in the hull.

The Diversion: The moment the sexual act is committed, the "Cargo" intended for your 2026 marriage or your 2030 business empire is diverted. It is moved from the "Surface of Manifestation" to the **"Underwater Vaults of the Abyss."**

Identifying Your Hijacked Assets: To recover your future, you must perform a **Judicial Audit** of what is missing. The Marine Kingdom specifically targets:

The Marital "Honey": The capacity for deep, soul-satisfying intimacy in your future marriage. This is why fornicators often feel "numb" or "bored" once they finally get married; the honey is sitting at the bottom of the sea.

The Financial "Current": The "River of Wealth" intended to fund your Kingdom assignments. The Marine Kingdom uses your sexual fluids as a "currency" to purchase your poverty. This is why false Prophets are always into fornication looking for sexual fluids at all coast, this is a spiritual "currency"

The Prophetic "Signal": Your ability to hear God clearly. Because the Marine Kingdom is a realm of "Fog" and "Liquid Sorcery," it drowns your spiritual ears in the noise of past lovers.

The "Warehouse" of the Deep: At the bottom of the sea, there are **Demonic Warehouses** (Job 41:31 "It makes the depths churn like a boiling caldron and stirs up the sea like a pot of ointment)."

Job, mentions the deep being like a "pot of ointment" or a boiling cauldron).

The Storage: Your hijacked future is stored there in "Spiritual Containers" labeled with your name and the "Legal Clause" that allowed the hijack (e.g., "Contract signed in Room 402, April 2024").

The Guards: These warehouses are guarded by "Monitoring Spirits" and "Marine Wardens" who ensure you stay in a state of "Dryness" on land while your "Water" is being used to power their kingdom. They will make even salvation to become so difficult because they are monitoring closely. This is why you need a praying mother, family member to stand in the gap and rescue souls like this.

Locating the Hijack via Dream Indicators: The Governor uses "Dream Intelligence" to locate the cargo.

The Indicator: If you constantly dream of being near large bodies of water, losing your luggage at a pier, or seeing your belongings "floating" just out of reach, these are **Judicial Evidence** that your future has been hijacked by marine entities.

The Spirit Spouse Signal: If you see a "Shadowy Figure" in your dreams claiming to be your husband or wife, that is the **Warden** of your hijacked cargo, making sure you don't form a holy merger on land.

The Executive Repossession Order: You do not "ask" the pirate for your goods back; you send a **Writ of Execution** from the Court of Heaven.

The Authority: Under the Law of Restitution, the thief must return what was stolen (Proverbs 6:31).

The Retrieval: You must command the **"Divine Divers"** of the Holy Spirit to go into the depths and bring up the "Containers of your Destiny."

The Governor's Verdict: Your future is not "gone"; it is **Hijacked.** It is sitting at the bottom of the sea, waiting for a Governor with the judicial authority to demand a "Surface Manifestation." You cannot have a clean bloodline if your "Cargo" is still in the hands of the Mother of Harlots.

The Executive Decree: "I stand in the Court of the Just Judge and I call for an Audit of my Destiny Ship! I identify the Cargo that was Hijacked through the bed of fornication. By the Gavel of Purity, I issue an **Executive Repossession Order** against the Marine Warehouses! I command every underwater vault: **Release My Marital Honey! Release My Financial Current! Release My Prophetic Signal!** I decree that my merchandise shall no longer sit at the bottom of the sea. I command the 'Divine Divers' to bring up my hijacked future now! I am no longer a 'Broken Ship'; I am a Restored Vessel of Light, In The name of Jesus!"

Chapter 6: The Transfer of Toxins

What Are You Taking into Your Marriage? The Hidden Baggage of Previous Unions

In the spiritual administration of a marriage, many couples believe they are starting with a "Clean Slate" on their wedding day. However, in the judicial realm, marriage is a **Merger of Two Estates**. If one or both estates have been previously compromised by the "Foundational Crack" of fornication, they are not just bringing themselves into the union; they are bringing a **Transfer of Toxins**. These are the "Invisible Passengers" and "Hidden Baggage" that cause unexplained turbulence in the homes of even the most well-meaning believers.

The Law of Spiritual Contamination (Haggai 2:12-13)

"If someone carries consecrated meat in the fold of their garment, and that fold touches some bread or stew, some wine, olive oil or other food, does it become consecrated?"
The priests answered, "No." **13** Then Haggai said, "If a person defiled by contact with a dead body touches one of these things, does it become defiled?"
"Yes," the priests replied, "it becomes defiled."

The Asymmetry of Defilement: Holiness is not automatically transferred by proximity, but **defilement is. The Toxic Touch:** When you enter a holy marriage after a history of "Illegal Mergers," the "Uncleanliness" of those previous unions does not vanish just because you are wearing a white dress or a tuxedo. Without a judicial purging, you are transferring the "Dead Tissue" of your past sexual altars into the "Living Body" of your new marriage.

The "Cargo of Strangers" (Psalm 144:11)

The Psalmist cries out: *"Rescue me and deliver me from the hand of foreigners, whose mouth speaks lying words and whose right hand is a right hand of falsehood."*

The Invisible Third Party: Every person you have slept with has left a "Digital Footprint" in your soul. If those people were under the influence of marine spirits, addiction, or generational curses, those "Foreigners" are now legally attached to your intimacy.

The Baggage manifest: This "Hidden Baggage" manifests as:

Comparison Toxins: Uncontrollable mental comparisons between your spouse and past lovers.

Emotional Numbness: The inability to feel the "Honey" of the union because your "Emotional Nerve Endings" were cauterized in previous illegal fires.

Flashback Intrusions: Images of previous partners surfacing during intimate moments with your spouse, this is a **Monitoring Spirit** asserting its "Right of Occupancy."

The Transfer of "Marine Moisture" to the Marital Bed

As a **Governor of the Dry Ground**, you know that the Marine Kingdom thrives on "Wet foundations."

The Foundation Rot: If you take the "Toxins" of fornication into your marriage, you are introducing "Spiritual Dampness" into your new home. This is why some marriages feel "Cold" or "Heavy" for no apparent reason. It is the "Marine Fog" that followed one of the partners from the "Liquid Grave" of their past.

The Siphoning of Peace: These toxins act as a "Slow Leak" in the marriage. They siphon the peace and the finances of the new home to pay off the "Debts" incurred during the years of sexual rebellion.

The "Spirit Spouse" Baggage (Matthew 12:43-45)
When a person fornicates, they often attract a "Marine Warden" or a spirit spouse.
The Jealous Squatter: This entity does not leave just because you got a marriage license from the state. It views your earthly spouse as an **"Intruder." The Sabotage:** This "Hidden Baggage" is the source of "Unprovoked Rage" between couples, sexual dysfunction, and the "Barrenness of the Bed." The spirit spouse is fighting to protect its "Illegal Merger" by poisoning the legal one.

The Protocol of Decontamination (Leviticus 14)
In the Law, when a house was found with "Leprosy" (toxins) in the walls, the stones had to be scraped, and in some cases, removed.
The Judicial Scraping: You must go through a process of **Marital Decontamination.** This involves "naming the baggage" and performing a formal renunciation of every "Foreign Hand" that ever touched your estate.
The Blood Sprinkling: Just as the priest sprinkled blood to cleanse the house, you must apply the Blood of Jesus to the "Memory Centers" and "Intimacy Gates" of your soul to neutralize the toxins of previous unions.

The Governor's Verdict: You cannot have a "New Bloodline" while carrying "Old Toxins." Do not allow the "Mother of Harlots" to have a seat at your marriage table. You must perform an **Executive Audit** of your baggage and leave the "Foreigners" at the gate before you enter the chambers of your covenant.

The Executive Decree:

I stand as a Governor of Light and I refuse to carry the Toxins of the Deep into my marriage! I identify every 'Invisible Passenger' and every 'Hidden Baggage' from my past unions. By the Gavel of the Just Judge, I declare a **Total Decontamination** of my soul and body! I Sever the link between my marital bed and the altars of my past. I command every 'Foreign Hand' to let go of my destiny! I wash my foundation with the Blood of Jesus and I declare my marriage is a 'Toxin Free Zone,' governed by Holiness and Peace, In The Name Of Jesus!"

Suicidal Attachments: When Death Spirits Travel Through Sexual Chains

In the judicial architecture of the spirit, sex is a **Conduit**. It is a high-speed rail system designed to transport "Life" and "Covenant Blessings" between a husband and wife. However, when this system is accessed through the "Foundational Crack" of fornication, it becomes a pipeline for **Illegal Cargo**. One of the most lethal toxins transferred through these sexual chains is the **Spirit of Death**, manifesting as suicidal ideation, "soul-heaviness," and a mysterious desire to "expire" before one's time.

The Law of the "Death Merger" (Proverbs 7:22-23, 27)

The book of Proverbs provides a chilling judicial autopsy of a young man entering an illegal merger: *"All at once he followed her... till an arrow pierced his liver, like a bird rushing into a snare, little knowing it will cost him his life. Her house is a highway to the grave, leading down to the chambers of death."*

The Lethal Entry: The "Arrow" mentioned here is not physical; it is a **Spiritual Projectile**. When you fornicate with someone who carries a "Death Assignment" or is under a suicidal curse, that spirit uses the act of intimacy as a "Needle" to inject its venom into your liver (the seat of life and filtering).

The Highway to the Grave: Fornication doesn't just "feel bad", it creates a **Legal Path** (*Highway*) for the Spirit of Death to move from one bloodline into yours. You may enter the bed with "Lust," but you leave with a "Lien on your Life."

The Marine Connection: The "Drowning" Mind

As a **Governor of the Dry Ground**, you must recognize that the Marine Kingdom is a realm of "Submersion."

The Weight of the Water: Suicidal spirits traveling through sexual chains often manifest as a feeling of being "underwater." This is "Liquid Sorrow."

The Siphoning of the "Will to Live": During the illegal merger, the marine entity siphons your "Oxygen" (your hope and joy) and replaces it with the "Saltwater" of the abyss. This is why, after certain sexual encounters, an individual may feel an inexplicable "Dark Cloud" or a sudden, intrusive thought that "life is no longer worth living." You have touched a **Chamber of Death.**

The "Transfer of Liability" (Ezekiel 18:20)

While the Bible says the son shall not bear the iniquity of the father, the **Law of Union** (1 Corinthians 6:16) states that "the two shall become one."

The Ghost Debt: If you join yourself to a person whose ancestors made "Death Covenants" or who has a history of "Blood Sacrifices" (including abortions), you are legally co-signing their **Death Warrant**.

The Suicidal Chain: This is how "Generational Suicide" travels. A person who was never suicidal begins to contemplate "the end" because they have merged with a partner who carries a "Death

Attachment." The spirit sees the new foundation and attempts to "Sink the Ship" before it reaches the harbor of Life.

Identifying the "Death Pulse": As a Governor, you must perform a **Diagnostic Audit** if you have a history of sexual compromise. Signs of a "Death Attachment" include:

Nightmare Indicators: Dreams of being buried alive, swimming in black water, or being "invited" to the grave by a former lover.

The "Expire" Urge: A sudden loss of interest in your "First Book" or your "Manuscripts," replaced by a desire to "just give up."

The Monitoring Shadow: Feeling a cold presence in your bedroom, this is the "Warden of the Grave" checking on its illegal cargo.

Breaking the Death Chain (Isaiah 28:18)

The Just Judge has issued a **Stay of Execution**: *"Your covenant with death will be annulled, and your agreement with Sheol will not stand."*

The Judicial Annulment: You must stand in the Court of Heaven and demand that the "Covenant of Death" formed during fornication be **Annulled.**

Severing the Chain: You must use the Gavel to strike the "Sexual Pipeline" that connected you to that toxic source. You must "Vomit up" the saltwater of the deep and breathe in the "Ruach" (Breath) of God.

The Governor's Verdict: You cannot enter your "Marriage of 2026, 2029, 2031" while tethered to a "Grave of 2024." Every suicidal thought is a **Legal Argument** from the Marine Kingdom claiming your life because of an illegal merger. You must silence the argument by the Blood of Jesus and re-establish your "Right to Life."

The Executive Decree:

"I stand as a Governor of Light and I strike the Gavel against every **Spirit of Death** attached to my soul through previous unions! I renounce every 'Covenant with the Grave' I formed in the bed of fornication. I command the 'Suicidal Chains' to **Shatter** by the Fire of the Lord! I disconnect my liver, my heart, and my mind from every 'Death Attachment.' I am NOT a highway to the grave; I am a Temple of the Living God! I choose **Life**! I choose my Future! I choose the 'Dry Ground'! Every marine entity of suicide, **Pack Your Baggage And Vacate My Estate, In The Name of Jesus!"**

Part III: The Marital Impact & Legacy Leakage

Chapter 7: Married Strangers

Why Spirits "Rattle" After the Wedding: The Emergence of Hidden Rivalries

In the judicial realm, the wedding day is the moment a **Legal Throne** is established. However, for many, the "Honeymoon Phase" is abruptly interrupted by an atmospheric shift, a sudden coldness, unprovoked arguments, or a feeling that you are sleeping next to a stranger. As a **Governor**, you must understand that the "rattling" you hear is the sound of **Hidden Rivalries**. These are the spirits attached to previous "Illegal Mergers" that remained silent during the dating phase but have now been "activated" by the legal establishment of your marriage.

The "Legal Protest" in the Spirit Realm

When you were dating or fornicating, the Marine Kingdom was silent because you were "operating within their jurisdiction." You were a customer on their trading floor. But the moment you say "I do" in a holy covenant, you have **Defected to Zion**.

The Squatter's Rights: Spirits from past unions view your marriage as an "Illegal Eviction." They believe they have "Seniority" because they occupied your foundation first.

The Rattling: Matthew 12:44 describes a spirit saying, *"I will return to my house from which I came."* When these spirits see you trying to build a new, holy life, they "rattle" the cage of your emotions and your peace to remind you of the "Unfinished Business" in the Deep.

The Emergence of the "Third Party" Shadow

In a holy marriage, the "Two become One." But when toxins have been transferred, it is often **"Three (or more) becoming One."**

Hidden Rivalries: You may find yourself arguing with your spouse, but the *nature* of the argument feels "foreign." You are not fighting with your husband or wife; you are fighting the **Residual Personality** of someone they (or you) slept with years ago.

The Comparison Demon: This spirit whispers comparisons into the mind. It highlights the spouse's flaws and magnifies the "false sweetness" of a past illegal union. This is a strategic "Rattle" designed to make you regret your covenant and look back toward "Sodom."

The Jealousy of the Marine Warden (Numbers5:14)

In the spiritual administration of marriage, we must identify one of the most persistent "Squatters" that refuses to leave after the foundation has been cracked: the **Marine Warden**. In many circles, this is identified as a "Spirit Spouse" a high level marine entity that claims a "Common Law" right to your vessel based on past illegal mergers. This entity does not just want to visit; it wants to **monopolize** your intimacy and sabotage the "Marital Honey" God intended for your union.

The Spirit of Jealousy: The Warden's Claim

The Scripture speaks of a **"Spirit of Jealousy"** (**Numbers 5:14**). While this can manifest between humans, in the spirit realm, it is the signature of the Marine Warden who feels "cheated on" when you enter a Holy Covenant.

The Illegal Claim: This entity views every past act of fornication as a "Signing Ceremony." Even though you have moved on physically, the Warden still holds a "Lien" against your loins in the spiritual archives.

The Sabotage of Intimacy: The "Rattling" of this spirit often occurs in the bedroom. Because the Warden previously enjoyed "Access" to your vessel through compromise, it now manifests as **Sexual**

Apathy, Pain, or Dysfunction. It attempts to make the physical union of marriage a place of "Frustration" rather than a place of "Fortification."

The Goal: Drowning the Joy

The Warden is a thief of sweetness. Its primary objective is to ensure that the "Honey" of your new marriage is never tasted.

The "Wet Bed" Strategy: The Marine Kingdom wants to keep the marital bed "Wet" not with the lubricant of grace, but with the **Tears of Frustration**. By introducing coldness or dysfunction, the Warden seeks to keep the couple as "Married Strangers."

The Siphoning of Synergy: When a husband and wife cannot connect intimately, their "Spiritual Synergy" is broken. They lose the power to "chase ten thousand" (Deuteronomy32:30) because their focus is consumed by the "War in the Walls."

Numbers 5:14

"If the spirit of jealousy comes upon him and he becomes jealous of his wife, who has defiled herself..."

The Spiritual Reality:

The Defilement Trigger: Notice that the spirit of jealousy is triggered by **Defilement**. Fornication is the "Scent" that attracts the Warden.

The Persistent Warden: This entity is a "Legalist." It argues that because you "Merged" with the deep in your past, you no longer have the right to be "One" with your spouse in the present.

The Verdict: You are telling the next generation: *"Do not invite a Warden into your future! Every 'casual' merger is a 'Marriage Proposal' to a marine entity. If you give them access today, they will try to sabotage your joy tomorrow. Keep your vessel 'Exclusive' for the King and your future spouse!"*

A Watchman's "Warden Eviction" Decree

"I strike the Gavel and I issue a 'Final Eviction Notice' to every Marine Warden claiming a right to our bloodline! I invoke the Blood of Jesus and I declare that every 'Illegal Marriage' signed in the bed of fornication is **Null** and **Void!**

"I 'Veto' the Spirit of Jealousy! I command every 'Marine Lien' against the loins of my children to be **Torn and Consumed** by the Fire of God! I decree that the 'Marital Honey' of their future unions is **Protected** and shall **Not** be siphoned by any aquatic spirit!

"I command every manifestation of sexual apathy, pain, and dysfunction to **Cease and Desist**! I decree that the 'Bed of the Covenant' shall be **Undefiled and Full** of the Joy of the Lord! No longer shall the bed be 'Wet' with tears; it shall be 'Salt Free' and 'Dry' from the influence of the abyss!

"We break the 'Common Law' of the deep! We establish the 'Covenant Law' of Zion! I decree a 'Total Separation' from the spirit spouses of the marine kingdom! The siphons are cut, the Warden is evicted, and the Marriage is WHOLE! In Jesus' Name!"

Why They Wait Until *After* the Wedding

A common question in the Governor's Council is: *"Why was everything fine while we were dating?"* **The Bait and Switch:** The enemy is a strategist. He will not "rattle" while you are fornicating because he wants you to stay in that sin. He waits until you are **Legally Bound** in marriage to strike, because now the "Disaster" carries more weight. He wants to turn your "Testimony" into a "Trial."

The Activation of the Lien: Now that you have assets (a home, a shared name, a joint destiny), the creditors of the Deep show up to collect on the "Debts" of your youth.

Silencing the Rattle: The Judicial Eviction

You cannot "talk" these spirits out of your marriage. You must **Evict** them through a formal Judicial Protocol.

Identify the "Rattle": Where is the tension coming from? Is it a "Death Attachment"? A "Comparison Spirit"? A "Marine Warden"?

The Writ of Quiet Enjoyment: In natural law, a tenant has the right to "Quiet Enjoyment" of their property. In the Kingdom, you have the right to a peaceful marriage. You must present your **Marriage Covenant** as a "Superior Deed" that overrides all previous "Illegal Leases."

The Governor's Verdict

You are not "incompatible" with your spouse; you are being **Interrupted** by your past. The "Stranger" in your bed is the shadow of a previous merger that hasn't been legally severed. You must strike the Gavel and declare that the "Registry of Strangers" is closed.

The Executive Decree:

"I stand in my office as a Governor and I address every 'Rattling Spirit' in my marriage! I identify the 'Hidden Rivalries' and the 'Marine Wardens' that followed me into this covenant. By the Gavel of the Just Judge, I declare: **You Have No Legal Standing Here!** I present the Blood of Jesus as the total payment for every past debt. I revoke every 'Squatter's Right' claimed by previous lovers or marine entities. I command the 'Stranger' to vacate my home, my mind, and my bed! I declare a 'Season of Quiet Enjoyment' over my union. My marriage is a 'Closed Estate' no third parties allowed, **In The Name of Jesus!"**

Guilt, Shame, and Dream Indicators: The Persistent Shadow of the Spirit Spouse

In the judicial council of a Governor, **Guilt and Shame** are not just "emotions"; they are **Atmospheric Toxins** used by the Marine Kingdom to maintain a legal "Shadow" over your life. While the Spirit Spouse (the Warden) may have been "evicted" from the physical bed, it often seeks to remain as a "Mental Squatter," using the baggage of your past to keep you from walking in the authority of your mandate.

The Weaponization of Shame (Zechariah\ 3:1-3)

The Scripture gives us a courtroom scene: *"Then he showed me Joshua the high priest standing before the Angel of the Lord, and Satan standing at his right hand to oppose him... Now Joshua was clothed with filthy garments."*

The "Filthy Garment" of Fornication: Shame is the "Filthy Garment" the Spirit Spouse forces you to wear. It whispers that you are "soiled goods" and that your past illegal mergers have permanently disqualified you from a holy marriage.

The Opposition: The goal of this shame is to keep you from standing "Righteously" before the Lord. If the Warden can make you feel "Dirty," you will not strike the Gavel with authority. Shame is the "Saltwater" that prevents your foundation from ever fully drying.

The Anatomy of "Spirit Spouse" Dreams

In the judicial oversight of your Kingdom Estate, you must understand that the enemy is a persistent "Legalist." When a Marine Warden (Spirit Spouse) loses its legal right to your physical body through your decision to walk in holiness, it does not always retreat immediately. Instead, it moves its operations to the **Dream Gate**. The goal is to maintain a "Shadow Covenant" in the subconscious, hoping to keep a "Backdoor" open into your foundation.

The Dream Indicators: Identifying the Shadow Strike

The Dream Gate is a sensitive entry point where the Marine Kingdom attempts to "Renew the Lease" on your soul while your conscious mind is at rest. You must be able to decode these indicators to maintain the security of your Estate:

The Recurring "Ex": This involves constantly dreaming of intimacy with a former partner. In the spirit, this is rarely the actual person; it is a **Marine Entity wearing a "Mask."** The entity uses the image of your past compromise to reinforce the old merger and trick your soul into "re-signing" the contract of the deep.

The Underwater Wedding: Dreaming of a wedding ceremony in a dark, watery place, or marrying a figure whose face is obscured, is a high-level **Infiltration Attempt**. The Warden is trying to establish a "Common Law" marriage in the spirit realm to prevent you from experiencing the full "Marital Honey" of your physical union.

Lost Rings or Torn Veils: Dreams where your wedding dress is dirty, your veil is torn, or your wedding ring is missing are **Psychological Strikes**. The enemy is trying to breed a "Spirit of Fear," making you believe that your "Marriage Must Hold" mandate is failing or that you are "too defiled" to be a bride of Zion.

The Judicial Response: Closing the Subconscious Gate

A Governor does not wake up from such dreams in fear; a Governor wakes up with a **Restraining Order**.

The Dream Audit: You must teach your children that dreams are "Evidence." If the enemy is showing up in the Dream Gate, it means there is still a "Spiritual Scent" or a "Tear in the Fence" that needs to be addressed through renunciation.

The Power of the Blood: The subconscious must be "Sanitized" by the Word of God. Just as you lock the doors of your house at night, you must "Lock the Dream Gate" with the Blood of the Lamb before you sleep.

Job 33:14–17

"For God may speak in one way, or in another, yet man does not perceive it. In a dream, in a vision of the night, when deep sleep falls upon men... Then He opens the ears of men, and seals their instruction. In order to turn man from his deed, and conceal pride from man."

The Spiritual Reality:

The "Sealing of Instruction" Clause: God uses dreams to give "Instructions" for your protection. If you see a "Spirit Spouse" in a dream, God is not trying to scare you; He is **Opening Your Ears** to the fact that a squatter is on the property.

The Turning Mechanism: The dream is a "Warning Bell" intended to **Turn you from the deed**. It is an invitation to rise up and "Cancel the Lease."

The Verdict: You are telling the next generation: *"Your dreams are not just 'movies'; they are 'Legal Briefs'! If the enemy shows up as an 'Ex' or an 'Underwater Groom,' do not be afraid. Wake up and serve him an Eviction Notice! Your subconscious belongs to the King!"*

A Watchman's "Dream gate" Security Decree

"I strike the Gavel and I establish 'Sentinel Angels' at the Dream Gates of my children! I invoke Job 33:15 and I decree that their sleep shall be Sweet and their dreams shall be filled with the Instructions of Zion!

"I 'Veto' every 'Underwater Wedding' and every 'Shadow Contract' attempted in the night! I command every Marine Entity wearing the 'Mask of the Ex' to be Unmasked and **Consumed by The Fire Of God**! I decree that my seed shall NOT resign any old mergers in their sleep!

"I command every 'Torn Veil' and 'Lost Ring' in the spirit to be replaced by the 'Garment of Praise' and the 'Ring of Authority'! I decree that our subconscious is a 'Restricted Zone' for the Marine Warden!

"I 'Seal' the Dream Gate with the Blood of the Lamb! I decree that the 'Water of the Deep' cannot enter the 'Dry Ground' of our rest! We wake up in Victory, we sleep in Peace, and our Estate is Secure! In Jesus' Name!"

Guilt as a "Monitoring Frequency"

Guilt acts as a "Radio Signal" that allows the Spirit Spouse to find you.

The Frequency Lock: As long as you carry "Secret Guilt," you are still "Vibrating" at the frequency of the Deep. This allows the Marine Warden to stay attached to your "Shadow."

The Siphoning of Confidence: A Governor without confidence cannot rule. Guilt siphons your "Commanding Voice," making your prayers feel hollow and your manuscripts feel like "just paper."

The "Mirror of the Past" vs. The "Mirror of the Word"

The Spirit Spouse holds up a "Mirror of the Past," showing you every "Entry Point of Decay" you ever allowed.

The Judicial Switch: You must stop looking into the "Marine Mirror" and start looking into the **Law of Liberty** (James 1:25).

The Cleansing of the Dream Gate: To stop the dreams, you must apply the "Blood of the Lamb" to your subconscious mind. You must declare that your "Night Territory" is now a **No-Fly Zone** for marine entities.

Striking the Gavel of "No Condemnation" (Romans 8:1)

"There is therefore now no condemnation to those who are in Christ Jesus..."

The Final Verdict: Condemnation is a "Foreign Law." As a Governor, you only recognize the **Judicial Verdict of the Cross**.

Evicting the Shadow: You must formally renounce the "Shame Attachment." You must tell the Spirit Spouse: *"You are using a canceled debt to harass a debt-free Governor!"*

The Governor's Verdict:
The "Shadow" of the Spirit Spouse only has power as long as you believe the lie of your "Unworthiness." The guilt you feel is a **Marine Fraud**. You have been washed, you have been sanctified, and you have been justified. Strike the Gavel and command the Shadow to dissolve in the Light of your destiny.

The Executive Decree:
"I stand in the Court of Heaven and I strike the Gavel against the **Spirit of Shame!** I renounce every 'Filthy Garment' placed upon me by the Mother of Harlots. I address the Spirit Spouse: **Your Lease Is Expired!** I am no longer 'Soiled Goods'; I am a Royal Priest and a Governor of Light. I apply the Blood of Jesus to my Dream Gate. I command every recurring image of past lovers to Be Blotted Out! I refuse the 'Mirror of the Past.' I am a New Creation with a New Foundation. I walk in 'No Condemnation,' and I declare my soul is **Dry, Holy, And Free, In The name of Jesus!"**

Chapter 8: The Generational Leak

Transferring Illegal Covenants: How Fornication Becomes a Bloodline Curse

In the spiritual administration of a family, the bloodline is intended to be a **Conduit of Blessing**. However, when a Governor engages in sex before marriage, they are not just making a personal choice; they are opening a **Sluice Gate** in the spirit. Fornication acts as a "Legal Virus" that enters the genetic and spiritual code of a bloodline, ensuring that the "Foundational Crack" of the parent becomes the "Gaping Hole" of the child.

The Law of the "Iniquity Visitation" (Exodus 20:5)

The Scripture establishes a judicial precedent: *"...visiting the iniquity of the fathers upon the children to the third and fourth generations of those who hate Me."*

The Iniquity Leak: While "Sin" is the act, "Iniquity" is the **Structural Bent** or the "Legal Liability" that remains. Sex before marriage creates a "Wet Spot" in the DNA.

The Generational Transfer: Because the act of sex is a **Covenant Mechanism**, the "Marine Debt" incurred during the union is "Auto Debted" from the accounts of the next generation. This is why children often struggle with the exact same "Sexual Pulls" or "Marital Delays" as their parents, the debt was never settled in the Court of Heaven.

The "Genetic Pager" of the Marine Kingdom

As a **Governor**, you must understand that the Marine Kingdom uses blood as a **Tracking System**.

The Signature of the Deep: When an illegal merger occurs, a "Digital Signature" of that marine entity is stamped onto the blood.

The Call of the Deep: Years later, when the child of that union reaches maturity, the Marine Kingdom "Pages" them. They release a "Sonar Frequency" that triggers a sudden, unexplainable urge to fornicate or rebel. The child is simply "Responding to the Leak" in their foundation that was created before they were born.

The "Covenant of the Unborn" (Hebrews7:9-10)

The Bible presents a mystery: *"Even Levi, who receives tithes, paid tithes through Abraham, so to speak, for he was still in the loins of his father when Melchizedek met him."*

The Loins as a Legal Vault: Just as Levi "paid tithes" while still in Abraham, your future children are "signing contracts" while they are still in your loins.

The Hijacked Seed: If you fornicate, you are essentially "Trading the Seed" of your marriage on a Marine Trading Floor. You are giving the enemy a **Legal Lien** on your children's purity before they have even been conceived. This is the definition of a **Legacy Leak**.

Breaking the "Vicious Cycle" of the Bloodline

In the spiritual administration of your lineage, a bloodline curse is not a mysterious "bad luck" streak; it is a **Recurring Judicial Verdict**. It is a repetitive claim in the spirit realm where the enemy argues: *"I had a legal right to the father's foundation; therefore I have a right to occupy the son's Estate."* If left unchallenged, this verdict becomes a "Vicious Cycle" that siphons the glory of every subsequent generation before they can reach their peak.

The Power of the New Covenant: The "Stay of Execution"

As a Governor of the Dry Ground, you are not a victim of your history; you are a **Legislator** of your future.

The Legislative Override: The New Covenant is a "Superior Constitution." It provides you with the authority to issue a **"Stay of**

Execution" over your bloodline. This means you can legally halt the enforcement of ancient verdicts that were passed down due to the compromises of your ancestors.

The New Title Deed: Through the Blood of Christ, you have received a new "Title Deed" to your life. The old "Liens" held by the marine kingdom are no longer valid if you choose to enforce the new terms of your citizenship in Zion.

The Bloodline Audit: Identifying the "Pattern of the Leak"

To stop a cycle, you must first identify its **Frequency**. You must perform a "Bloodline Audit" a clinical and spiritual examination of your history.

The Audit Checklist: Look back at the history: the recurring divorces, the "Babies out of Wedlock," the secret sexual addictions, and the patterns of "sinking" just before success.

Locating the Leak: These are not coincidences; they are the **"Indicators of the Leak."** Once you identify the pattern, you have identified the "Pipe" through which the marine kingdom has been siphoning the strength of your family.

The Judicial Severance: Suturing the DNA

Once the leak is identified, it must be closed through **Judicial Severance**. You must use the "Gavel of the Spirit" to declare that the "Iniquity of the Loins" stops with you.

Suturing the Wound: Think of your DNA as a spiritual "Vessel." The compromises of the past created "Wounds" in that vessel where the glory leaks out. You must use the Blood of the Lamb as a "Spiritual Suture" to stitch the DNA back together, making it a "Closed System" once again.

The New Decree: You are declaring to the spirit realm: *"The debt of my fathers is settled! The lease of the marine kingdom has expired! I am the generation that disconnects from the cycle and reconnects to the Throne!"*

Ezekiel 18:2-3

"What do you mean by repeating this proverb concerning the land of Israel, 'The fathers have eaten sour grapes, and the children's teeth are set on edge'? 'As I live,' says the Lord God, 'this proverb shall no more be used by you in Israel.'"

The Spiritual Reality:

The "Sour Grapes" Clause: The proverb described a **Generational Debt** where children suffered for the parents' choices.

The "No More" Mandate: God Himself issued a "Cease and Desist" order against generational cycles. He declared that every soul stands on its own "Estate."

The Verdict: You are telling the next generation: *"You don't have to 'pay' for the sour grapes of your ancestors! The cycle ends here! You are a 'New Foundation' believer, and the old verdicts have no power to prosecute your future!"*

A Watchman's "Bloodline Disconnect" Decree

"I strike the Gavel and I authorize a 'Bloodline Audit' over our entire history! I invoke Ezekiel 18:3 and I decree that the 'Proverb of the Sour Grapes' shall **No Longer** be used against my seed! The 'Iniquity of the Loins' is **Severed And Reversed** by the Blood of the Lamb!

"I issue a 'Stay of Execution' over every recurring pattern of divorce, fornication, and delay! I 'Veto' the claims of the marine kingdom against my children's loins! I decree that the 'Debt of the Fathers' is **Paid In Full** by the Price of the Cross!

"I 'Suture the Wound' in our DNA! I command every leak in our family vessel to be **Closed!** I decree that my seed is a 'Sanitized Generation' free from the ghosts of the past and the claims of the deep! We are disconnecting from the 'Vicious Cycle' and connecting to the 'Virtuous Cycle' of Zion!

"We pass down a 'Clear Title'! We pass down a 'Full Treasury'! The old verdict is **Overruled,** the new covenant is **Enforced,** and our bloodline is **Free!** In Jesus' Name!"

Establishing a "Dry Foundation" for the Next Generation

Your goal is to ensure that your future marriage is a **"Covenant of the Dry Ground."**

The Firewall of Purity: By repenting and closing the "Fornication Entry Point," you are building a **Firewall** around your future children.

The New Registry: You are de registering your bloodline from the Marine Registry of Harlots and registering it in the **Book of the Generations of the Righteous**.

The Governor's Verdict:

Fornication is the "Silent Leak" that drowns the next generation before they can swim. You are not just fighting for your own purity; you are fighting for the **Structural Integrity of your Posterity**. Do not let the "Mother of Harlots" claim your grandchildren through a mistake you make today.

The Executive Decree:

"I stand in the Court of Heaven as a Governor of my Bloodline! I identify every 'Generational Leak' created by the sin of fornication in my ancestry and in my own life. By the Gavel of the Just Judge, I declare: **The Leak Is Closed!** I apply the Blood of Jesus to the 'Loins of my Future.' I revoke every legal claim the Marine Kingdom holds over my unborn children. I Sever the 'Genetic Pager' of the Deep! I decree that my future marriage shall be a source of Life, not a conduit of curses. My children shall be 'Royal Priests' with a 'Dry Foundation,' **In the Name Of Jesus!"**

Family Chaos and Divorce

The Natural Harvest of a Corrupted Foundation: In the judicial administration of the spirit, **Chaos** is not an accident; it is a **Manifestation of Legal Disorder**. When a foundation is built upon the "Foundational Crack" of fornication, the resulting "Family Chaos" and "Divorce" are not merely emotional failures, they are the **Natural Harvest** of a seed planted in the wrong soil. As a Governor, you must understand that if the Marine Kingdom has a "Lien" on the foundation, it will eventually sue for the "Liquidation" of the entire estate.

The Law of the Harvest (Galatians 6:7-8)

The Scripture is a book of Spiritual Agronomy: *"Do not be deceived, God is not mocked; for whatever a man sows, that he will also reap. For he who sows to his flesh will of the flesh reap corruption..."*

The Sowing of the Flesh: Sex before marriage is a "Sowing to the Flesh." It is the act of planting the "Seed of Rebellion" into the "Soil of the Future."

The Harvest of Corruption: Corruption means "decay" or "ruin." Divorce is the ultimate "Ruin" of a covenant. When a couple marries on a foundation of fornication, they have already "Pre Sown" the seeds of their own separation. The chaos that erupts three years into the marriage is simply the "Sprout" of the illegal seed planted three years *before* the marriage.

The "Marine Squatter" and the Chaos of the Home: As a **Governor of the Dry Ground**, you know that the Marine Kingdom hates the "Dry Order" of a holy home.

The Entry Point: Fornication gives marine entities "Visitor Passes" into the future family. Once the wedding is over, these entities refuse to leave. They become "Squatters" in the spiritual atmosphere of the house.

The Manufacturing of Chaos: These spirits manufacture "Unprovoked Rage," "Silent Treatments," and "Financial Leakage." Their goal is to make the environment so "Wet" with tears and strife that the "Dry Ground" of the marriage license can no longer sustain the structure. Chaos is the "Hammer" the enemy uses to turn the "Crack" into a "Canyon."

Divorce as a "Judicial Foreclosure"

In the natural world, if you don't pay your mortgage, the bank forecloses on your house. In the spirit world, if you "purchased" your pleasure through fornication, the Marine Kingdom eventually comes to **Foreclose on your Peace.**

The Debt Collector: The Spirit Spouse or the Marine Warden acts as the "Bailiff." They argue in the Court of Heaven: *"This person traded their marital virtue to us years ago; therefore, this marriage is an illegal construction on our territory."*

The Eviction (Divorce): Divorce is the enemy's way of "Evicting" God's presence from a family. It is the final harvest of a foundation that was never judicially "Dried and Set" through deep repentance and foundational deliverance.

The "Broken Hedge" and the Serpent's Bite (Ecclesiastes10:8)

In the judicial administration of a Kingdom Estate, the "Hedge" is the primary security infrastructure of the household. It is a spiritual perimeter designed to keep the blessings in and the predators out. However, many believers operate with a **"Security Breach"** they are unaware of. They wonder why "family chaos" persists in their lives despite their prayers. The answer is often found in the structural integrity of their perimeter.

The Protective Hedge: The Marital Perimeter Marriage is designed to be a "Walled Garden," a hedge of protection. But when sex occurs before marriage, you are attempting to enjoy the "fruit" of the garden while **"Breaking the Hedge"** before it is even fully established.

The Premature Breach: Fornication is not just an act; it is a "Forced Entry." It creates a gap in the spiritual fencing of your future marriage before the "Marriage License" is even issued.

The Structural Weakness: When you finally enter marriage with a history of unrepented compromises, you are moving into a house with a "Broken Wall." The perimeter is not a solid circle of protection; it is a series of "Gaps" held together by hope rather than holiness.

The Serpent's Bite: The Future Strike

The Scripture warning is precise: *"Whoever breaks through a wall, a hedge, will be bitten by a serpent"* (**Ecclesiastes 10:8**).

The Gap of Divorce: The "Serpent" of divorce, infidelity, and family chaos does not always attack from the front gate. It finds the **"Previous Gap"** the hole in the hedge created by past fornications. This is why many "Good Christians" experience sudden, unexplained collapses in their marriages; they were "Born Again," but they never **Repaired the Hedge** of their foundation.

The Hidden Entry: The serpent is a patient predator. It crawls through the gap you left open ten years ago and strikes the "Marital Peace" of today. If the old breach is not "Gavelled" and sealed through renunciation, the serpent still has a "Legal Right of Way" to enter the house.

Ecclesiastes 10:8

"He who digs a pit will fall into it, and whoever breaks through a wall will be bitten by a serpent."

The Spiritual Reality:

The "Breached Wall" Clause: A wall is meant to be a barrier. Once a "Breach" is made through a sexual merger, the wall is compromised for *anyone* in the spirit realm to enter.

The "Bitten" Penalty: The "Bite" is the injection of spiritual venom bitterness, coldness, and confusion into the family unit.

The Verdict: You are telling the next generation: *"Do not break the hedge of your future home today! Every compromise is a 'Hole' you are digging for yourself. If you have already broken the wall, do not just 'move on'; you must REBUILD and RE SEAL the gap before the serpent finds it!"*

A Watchman's "Hedge-repair" Decree

"I strike the Gavel and I authorize a 'Perimeter Inspection' over the households of my bloodline! I invoke Ecclesiastes 10:8 and I decree that every 'Broken Hedge' created by past fornication is being **Rebuilt** by the Power of the Holy Ghost!

"I 'Veto' the Serpent's Bite! I command every serpent of divorce, chaos, and infidelity that crawled through an old gap to **Get Out Now!** I 'Seal' the gaps in the hedge with the Blood of the Lamb and the Fire of Repentance!

"I decree that my children will **Not** enter marriage with 'Broken Walls'! I command every 'Previous Gap' to be closed and reinforced! I 'Suture' the breaches of the past so the venom of the deep cannot infect the peace of the future!

"Our hedges are 'Thick with Thorns' of Fire! Our walls are 'High with Holiness'! We are not a 'Breached City'; we are a 'Fortified Estate'! The serpent is evicted, the wall is repaired, and the Hedge is **Whole**! In Jesus' Name!"

Closing the Gap: The Governor's Restoration Protocol

To prevent the "Natural Harvest" of divorce, you must perform a **Judicial Intervention.**

The Uprooting: You must go into the "Field of your Foundation" and uproot the "Seeds of the Flesh" before they reach full maturity. This is done through specific renunciation of every illegal merger.
The Re Pouring of the Foundation: You must ask the Just Judge to "Re Pour" the concrete of your relationship with the "Blood of the Covenant." You must declare that your marriage is built on **Mount Zion**, which cannot be moved by the "Waves of the Sea."

The Governor's Verdict

Chaos is a signal that the "Owners of the Deep" are trying to reclaim their property. Divorce is not your destiny; it is a "Harvest" that can be **Aborted** by the power of the Gavel. Strike the Gavel today and declare that the "Season of Corruption" is over.

The Executive Decree:

"I stand as a Governor of my Estate and I strike the Gavel against the **Harvest of Chaos!** I identify every seed of fornication planted in my past and I command it to be **Uprooted** by the Fire of God! I revoke the 'Marine Lien' on my marriage and my family. I declare that the 'Serpent of Divorce' shall Not bite my household! I am repairing the hedge today by the Blood of Jesus. I refuse to reap corruption; I choose to reap Life and Peace. My foundation is DRY, my walls are STRONG, and my marriage shall **Hold, In The name of Jesus!"**

Chapter 9: The Normalized Evil

From Abortion to Children Out of Wedlock: How Open Doors Invite National Judgment

In the judicial administration of the Spirit, there is a phenomenon known as **"The Normalization of Abomination."** This occurs when a society moves from "committing a sin" to "codifying a sin" into its culture, laws, and everyday expectations. As a **Governor**, you must understand that sex before marriage is the **Gateway Gate** through which national judgment enters. When the "Foundational Crack" of fornication is ignored, it matures into the "Normalized Evils" of abortion and the dissolution of the family unit, triggering a response from the Court of Heaven that affects every level of human infrastructure.

The Family: The First Level of Annexation: The family is the basic "Judicial Unit" of the Kingdom.

The Erosion of Authority: When children are born out of wedlock, the "Structure of Authority" is compromised from Day One. The child is born into a "Jurisdictional Conflict" between two parents who have no covenantal bond.

The Altar of Convenience: Abortion is the "Sacrifice" offered to the Mother of Harlots to cover the "Evidence" of fornication. It is the blood shedding required to maintain the lie of "Freedom." This creates a **Blood Debt** over the family estate that silences the voice of blessing for generations.

The Church: The Compromised Sanctuaries: The Church is intended to be the **Garrison of Light**, but normalized evil turns it into a "House of Mixture."

The Silent Pulpit: When fornication is normalized in the pews, the "Prophetic Gavel" of the pulpit is broken. The Church loses its

Judicial Standing to rebuke the city because its own foundation is "Wet" with the same compromise.

The Spirit of Ichabod: The glory departs because the "Stewardship of the Vessel" has been traded for "Numerical Growth." A church full of fornicators is a church that has been annexed by the Marine Kingdom.

The Community and City: The Atmosphere of Defilement

A city is a collection of estates. When enough individual estates are corrupted by sex before marriage and abortion, the **Atmosphere of the City** changes.

The "Liquid Sorcery" of the Streets: The "Marine Fog" descends on the city, manifesting as increased crime, drug addiction, and mental health crises.

The Judicial Abandonment: In Ezekiel 8, God shows the prophet the "Abominations" in the secret chambers, which leads to God "departing far from His sanctuary." When a city normalizes sexual evil, the "Divine Shield" is lifted, leaving the city vulnerable to economic collapse and social unrest.

The Nation: The Invitation of National Judgment

National judgment is not God "losing His temper"; it is God **Respecting the Choice** of a nation to operate outside His Law.

The Breaking of the Staff: Isaiah 3 describes a nation under judgment: *"I will give children to be their princes, and babes shall rule over them."* This is the result of a generation that destroyed its "Father Infrastructure" through sexual lawlessness.

The Open Door to the East: National judgment often manifests as the loss of sovereignty. A nation that cannot "Govern its own Bodies" will eventually be governed by "Foreign Powers" who have no respect for their God.

The Results for the Future Generation (Hosea 4:6)

"Because you have forgotten the law of your God, I also will forget your children."

The Genetic Orphanhood: The next generation is born into a "Spiritual Desert." They inherit "Hijacked Futures" and "Empty Warehouses" because their parents spent their inheritance in the beds of Babylon.

The Identity Crisis: Without a "Clean Generation" to model after, the youth turn to the "Mother of Harlots" for their identity, leading to the explosion of gender confusion, addictions and suicidal attachments.

The Wrath of God: The Judicial Fire: The "Wrath of God" is the **Executive Fire** that consumes everything that is not built on the Rock.

The Divine Nausea: God says of the nations that practiced sexual abomination, *"the land vomited out its inhabitants"* (Leviticus 18:25). Wrath is the "Immune Response" of a Holy Earth against the "Bacteria of Sin."

The End of the Mercy Window: There is a "Window of Mercy" for repentance, but once evil is "Normalized," the window closes and the Gavel of Judgment falls.

The Importance of a Clean Generation (Psalm 24:3-4)

"Who may ascend into the hill of the Lord? ... He who has clean hands and a pure heart."

The Remnant Governors: God is looking for a **"Clean Generation"**, a group of individuals who refuse to drink the "Wine of Harlotry."

The Power of Restoration: A Clean Generation has the **Judicial Authority** to "Repair the Breach." One person standing in "Foundational Purity" can hold back the judgment of an entire city.

This is why your "Marriage" must be holy; it is not just for you, it is a **National Security Asset.**

The Governor's Verdict: Normalized evil is a "Slow Poison" that kills the nation from the bedroom upward. You must refuse to call "Normal" what God calls "Abominable." Your purity is your **Political Statement** in the Kingdom of God.

The Executive Decree:
"I stand as a Governor of Zion and I reject the Normalization of Evil! I strike the Gavel against the spirits of Abortion and Fornication in my lineage and my nation! I refuse to be a citizen of Babylon. I declare that I am part of the 'Clean Generation' that will ascend the Hill of the Lord. I apply the Blood of Jesus to the 'Gates of my City' and I demand a restoration of the Fear of the Lord. My future marriage shall be a 'Bastion of Purity' and a 'Garrison of Light' that pushes back the darkness of my nation, In the Name Of Jesus!"

Part IV: The Governor's Protocol For Restoration

Chapter 10: The Mandate of Repentance

Moving Beyond "New Identity" Excuses: The Necessity of Confession and Renunciation

In many modern circles, the concept of "New Identity" is often weaponized as a legal loophole to avoid the hard work of **Foundational Deconstruction**. People say, *"I'm a new creation; the past is gone,"* while they are still being harassed by the "Rattle" of the Spirit Spouse or the "Siphoning" of the Marine Kingdom. As a **Governor**, you must understand that while your *spirit* is made new at salvation, your **Foundational Estate** must still be judicially cleared of "Illegal Leases" and "Squatter's Rights." Repentance is not an admission of defeat; it is a **Mandate of Sovereignty.**

The Fallacy of the "Blanket New Identity"

The Scripture says, *"Old things have passed away; behold, all things have become new"* (2 Corinthians 5:17).

The Judicial Distinction: This verse refers to your **Citizenship and Nature**, but it does not automatically vacate the "Legal Liens" you placed on your body through previous covenants.

The Excuse Trap: Using "New Identity" as an excuse to avoid specific confession is like a man claiming he is a "New Homeowner" but refusing to pay the outstanding taxes or evict the squatters left by the previous owner. The squatters don't care about your "New Title"; they care about their **Un canceled Contract.**

The Necessity of Confession: The "Discovery" Phase (1John 1:9)

"If we confess our sins, He is faithful and just to forgive us our sins and to cleanse us from all unrighteousness."

The Strategic Detail: To "Confess" or to "Say the same thing as the Judge." You must stop calling fornication a "mistake" and call it **"Foundational Treason." Naming the Gateways:** General repentance (e.g., "Lord, forgive me for everything") lacks the judicial specificity to break a **Marine Connection.** You must confess the specific "Illegal Mergers" so the Court of Heaven can identify which "Bonds" to dissolve.

The Power of Renunciation: The Writ of Severance

If Confession is the *Discovery*, then **Renunciation** is the *Eviction.*

Breaking the Verbal Contract: Many sexual unions were sealed with words of "False Covenant" ("I will always love you," "We are one"). These words are **Binding Agreements** in the Deep.

The Judicial Severance: Renunciation is the formal act of "Un saying" those words. It is the Governor standing in the Court and declaring: *"I revoke my signature! I cancel the agreement! I renounce the merger!"* Without renunciation, the enemy argues that your "Heart" may be saved, but your "Word" still belongs to him.

Dismantling the "Mercy Only" Delusion: Many believers hide behind "God's Mercy" to avoid the pain of **Restitution and Deliverance. Mercy vs. Justice:** Mercy forgives the *sinner*, but Justice addresses the *sin's consequences.* God's Mercy gives you the *right* to stand in Court, but the Protocol of Repentance is how you *win the case.*

The Administrative Duty: As a Governor, it is your **Administrative Duty** to clean your own foundation. You cannot ask God to "be holy for you." You must use the Gavel of Repentance to purge your own Estate of its "Liquid Toxins."

The "Cleansing of the Conscience" (Hebrews 9:14)
The result of true repentance is the "Purging of the Conscience from dead works."
The Removal of the "Stain": When you move beyond excuses and enter deep confession, the "Blood of Christ" doesn't just forgive; it **Decontaminates.** It removes the "Scent" of the past lover that attracts the Spirit Spouse.
The Restoration of Command: Once the foundation is judicially cleared, your "Voice of Command" returns. You can no longer be "blackmailed" by the enemy's accusations because there is no "Evidence" left in the file.

The Governor's Verdict: Your "New Identity" is the **Authority** you use to repent, not the **Excuse** you use to avoid it. Do not let the "Mother of Harlots" keep a toehold in your life through the lie of "Automatic Deliverance." Use the Gavel today to perform a total Foundational Clearing.

The Executive Decree:
"I stand in my New Identity in Christ, and I refuse to use Grace as a cloak for foundational neglect! I bring every 'Illegal Merger' and 'Sexual Altar' of my past into the Court of Heaven for specific Confession. By the Gavel of the Just Judge, I **Renounce** every word, every fluid-covenant, and every soul tie I ever formed. I break the 'Spiritual Leases' held by the Marine Kingdom over my body. I am not 'Soiled Goods'; I am a Cleansed Governor! My foundation is being deconstructed and re poured with the Stone of Holiness. My past is not just 'ignored' it is Judicially Canceled, In the Name Of Jesus!"

The Cleansing Bath: Consecrating the Vessel for Kingdom Use
In the judicial protocol of the Governor, the "Cleansing Bath" is not a mere symbolic ritual; it is a **Total Systems Purge**. It is the transition from a "Corrupted Foundation" to a **"Sanctified Estate."** Once the legal renunciations have been filed, the vessel must undergo a deep consecration to ensure that the "Scent of the Deep" is completely replaced by the "Fragrance of the Altar." This is the process of making your vessel **"Meet for the Master's Use"**

2 Timothy 2:21"If a man therefore purge himself from these, he shall be a vessel unto honor, sanctified, and meet for the master's use, and prepared unto every good work.")

The Judicial Washing of the Water by the Word (Ephesians 5:26)
The Scripture describes Christ's method of restoration: *"...that He might sanctify and cleanse her with the washing of water by the word."*
The "Liquid Word": Just as the Marine Kingdom uses "Liquid Sorcery" to defile, the Kingdom of God uses the "Liquid Word" to decontaminate. As a Governor, you must immerse your mind in the Word until the "Saline Content" of your past experiences is neutralized.
The Flushing of the Memory: The Cleansing Bath involves a "Flushing" of the imagination. Every "Flashback" or "Image" of an illegal merger must be washed away by the constant application of Scripture until the "Screen of your Mind" is white and clean.

The Separation from "Common" Use Consecration to be **Set Apart**.

The End of Accessibility: A vessel in the "Cleansing Bath" is no longer "Open for Public Access." You must declare a **Moratorium on Intimacy** (if single) or a **Season of Consecration** (if married) to allow the "Spiritual Cement" of your foundation to dry without interruption.

The Removal of "Triggers": Part of the bath is removing physical and digital items that carry the "Scent" of past harlotry, gifts, photographs, or contacts that act as "Legal Tethering Points" to the Marine Kingdom.

The "Hyssop" Protocol (Psalm 51:7)

David, after his foundational crack with Bathsheba, cried out: *"Purge me with hyssop, and I shall be clean; wash me, and I shall be whiter than snow."*

The Judicial Detergent: Hyssop was used in the Law to sprinkle blood for the cleansing of lepers. In the spirit, this represents the **Specific Application of the Blood of Jesus** to the "Organs of Intimacy."

The Whiteness of Identity: The Cleansing Bath doesn't just "cover" the stain; it removes the **History of the Stain.** It restores the "Virginity of the Soul," allowing you to stand in your marriage as if the "Foundational Crack" never existed.

The Filling of the "Empty Chambers" (Matthew 12:44-45)

The "Cleansing Bath" leaves the house "Swept and Garnished," but the Governor knows that an empty house is a dangerous house.

Occupying the Estate: After the toxins are washed out, the "Chambers of the Heart" must be filled with **Kingdom Cargo**, the Fear of the Lord, Wisdom, and the Holy Spirit.

The Permanent Inhabitant: You must invite the Holy Spirit to take up **Exclusive Residency** in your vessel. You tell the Lord: *"This Estate is no longer for rent; it is Your Private Residence."*

The Fragrance of the Anointing (Ecclesiastes 9:8)
"Let your garments be always white, and let your head lack no oil."
The Result of the Bath: A cleansed vessel attracts a "New Oil." The "Oil of Joy" replaces the "Spirit of Heaviness" (the saltwater of the deep).
Kingdom Readiness: Once the vessel is "White" (Cleansed) and "Oiled" (Anointed), the Governor is ready for the "Governor's Verdict" manuscript and the marital mandate. You are no longer a "Harlot's Gateway"; you are a **Zion Gateway.**

The Governor's Verdict:
You cannot serve the King in a "Soiled Vessel." The "Cleansing Bath" is your transition from "Baggage" to "Blessing." Do not rush out of the bath. Let the Word soak into your foundation until every trace of the Marine Kingdom is dissolved.

The Executive Decree:
"I enter the 'Cleansing Bath' of the Word and the Blood! I command every 'Stain of the Past' to be dissolved now. I wash my eyes, my mind, and my body in the 'Liquid Word' of God. By the Gavel of the Just Judge, I declare that I am **Set Apart** for Kingdom Use. I am no longer 'Common' or 'Public'; I am the King's Private Estate. I apply the 'Hyssop of the Spirit' to my soul and I arise whiter than snow! I fill my chambers with the Fear of the Lord and I receive the 'New Oil' for my mandate. My vessel is holy, my foundation is dry, and I am Ready, In The name of Jesus!"

Chapter 11: Dismantling The Altar

The Judicial Order to Repent: Breaking Legal Demonic Claims

In the spiritual administration of an estate, an **Altar** is a legal "Point of Entry" where a human will meets a spiritual power. When you engage in sex before marriage, you have inadvertently constructed a **Sexual Altar** in the Deep. This altar serves as a permanent "Claim" that the Marine Kingdom holds against your future. As a **Governor**, you cannot simply "ignore" this altar; you must issue a **Judicial Order** to dismantle it, stone by stone, until the ground is cleared for your HOLY Covenant.

The Altar as a "Legal Base of Operations" (Judges 6:25-26)

Before Gideon could deliver Israel, the Lord gave him a specific judicial assignment: *"Take your father's young bull... pull down the altar of Baal that your father has, and cut down the wooden image that is beside it; and build an altar to the Lord your God on top of this rock in the proper arrangement."*

The Priority of Dismantling: You cannot build a "Throne" for your marriage until you pull down the "Altar" of your fornication.

The "Proper Arrangement": The Marine Kingdom uses the "Messy Arrangement" of secret sin to hide their altars. The Judicial Order to Repent brings these hidden altars into the Light, where they lose their legal structural integrity.

Breaking the "Liquid Contracts" of the Deep

In the Marine Kingdom, an altar is fueled by "Sacrifice" in this case, the sacrifice of your virtue and the exchange of fluids.

The Claim on the "Vessel": The enemy argues in the Court of Heaven: *"An altar was raised in Room X on Date Y; therefore, the vessel belongs to the Altar."*

The Judicial Order: Repentance is the "Legal Tool" that breaks the contract. When you repent with judicial precision, you are withdrawing the "Fuel" from the altar. Without the fuel of your agreement, the altar becomes **Unstable** and can be dismantled.

The Gavel Against the "Monitoring Spirits" (Job 1:7)

Every sexual altar has a "Warden" or a "Monitoring Spirit" assigned to it. These spirits "patrol" your life to ensure you never stray too far from the altar's influence.

The Rattle of the Chain: When you move toward your marriage mandate, these spirits "pull the chain" of the old altar, causing sudden fear, lustful flashbacks, or "Self-Sabotage."

The Restraining Order: As a Governor, your Judicial Order must include a **Permanent Restraining Order** against these wardens. You must declare: *"The Altar is gone, and your assignment is **Terminated!**"*

Uprooting the "Foundation Stones" of Harlotry

A sexual altar is built on "Stones" of specific experiences.

The Identification: You must identify the "Chief Stones" the key relationships or encounters that fundamentally shifted your character or opened the door to the "Mother of Harlots."

The Uprooting: You don't just "cover" the altar; you **Uproot** the stones. You renounce each specific "Illegal Merger" by name or by memory, casting those stones into the "Fire of Judgment."

Building the "Altar of the Rock" (Psalm 18:2)

Once the ground is cleared, you must immediately build a new altar, the **Altar of the Rock (Christ).**

The Sovereign Exchange: Where there was a "Sexual Altar," there must now be a **"Covenant Altar."**

The Dry Ground Foundation: This new altar is built on the "Dry Ground" of holiness. It is "Properly Arranged" to support the weight of the "Governor's Verdict"

The Governor's Verdict:
You cannot rule from a compromised foundation. The "Judicial Order to Repent" is your executive power to **Clear the Site.** Do not leave one stone standing, or the Marine Kingdom will use that single stone to rebuild the entire altar in your future home.

The Executive Decree:
"I stand in the Court of Heaven, and I issue a **Judicial Order To Dismantle** every sexual altar in my life! I pull down the altars of 'Baal' and the 'Mother of Harlots' constructed in the bed of fornication. By the Gavel of the Just Judge, I break every legal demonic claim! I command the 'Wardens of the Deep' to **Cease** their monitoring. I uproot the stones of my past and I cast them into the Fire. I am clearing the ground for my marriage Mandate! I build a new altar on the Rock of Christ a foundation that is **Dry, Holy, And Irreversible, In the Name Of Jesus!"**

Repossessing Your Destiny from the Marine Vaults
In the spiritual administration of your estate, the **Marine Vaults** are the deep level "Evidence Lockers" of the enemy. When the "Illegal Merger" was formed, your marital honey, financial oil, and prophetic manuscripts were not "destroyed" they were **Confiscated and Stored**. To the Marine Kingdom, these are "Spoils of War." As a **Governor**, your restoration is not complete until you move from the "Repentance" phase to the **"Repossession"** phase. You are not asking for a favor; you are executing a **Judicial Retrieval**.

The Location of the "Stolen Cargo" (Job 20:15)
The Scripture reveals the mechanics of this retrieval: *"He swallows down riches and vomits them up again; God will cast them out of his belly."*

The Belly of the Deep: The Marine Kingdom acts as a "Spiritual Glutton," swallowing the destinies of those who compromise. Your marriage, your finished project, and your business, career, wealthy are currently being held in the "Belly" (the Vaults) of aquatic princes.

The Judicial Emetic: Your Gavel and your Decree act as a spiritual emetic. You are forcing the Marine Kingdom to "Vomit" what it swallowed. You are declaring that the "Digestive Process" of the enemy, the attempt to turn your destiny into *their* energy, is legally stopped.

The "Writ of Restitution" (Proverbs 6:31)
The Law of the Kingdom is clear regarding theft: *"Yet if he is found, he must restore sevenfold; he may have to give up all the substance of his house."*

The Identification of the Thief: You must identify the "Marine Thief" who used the bed of fornication to steal your virtue.

The Sevenfold Demand: Because this was a criminal hijack of a Governor's Estate, you don't just demand your "cargo" back; you demand the **Interest**. You demand that the very wisdom the enemy tried to steal be returned to you sevenfold, becoming the "Deep Content" of your future manuscripts.

Breaking the "Seal of the Deep" (Revelation 5:5)
The Marine Vaults are protected by "Legal Seals" arguments based on your past sins.

The Opening of the Vault: Only the **Lion of the Tribe of Judah** has the authority to break these seals. When you stand in the Court of Heaven, you don't present your "good works"; you present the **Blood of the Lamb**.

The Blood as the Master Key: The Blood cancels the "sin code" that locked the vault. Once the seal is broken, the Marine Wardens have no legal authority to hold your assets. You are now authorized to enter the "Submerged Warehouse" and take back what is yours.

Repossessing the "Marital Honey" and "Prophetic Sharpness"

The Honey: Many who have fornicated feel "dry." You must specifically repossess the **Capacity for Delight**. You command the Marine Kingdom to release the sweetness intended for your union.

The Sharpness: The "Marine Fog" steals your ability to see the future. You repossess your "Prophetic Eyesight" from the liquid grave so you can see clearly.

The "Vomiting" of the Wealth of the Seas (Isaiah 60:5)

"...because the abundance of the sea shall be turned to you, the wealth of the Gentiles shall come to you."

The Wealth Transfer: This is the ultimate "Repossession Decree." The very kingdom that tried to bankrupt you through sexual "Trade" is now judicially forced to **Fund your Mandate.**

From Siphoning to Pouring: The "Pipe" that once siphoned your resources is now "Reversed." The assets of the Deep are being poured into your Estate to build the "Governor's Verdict."

The Governor's Verdict:

Your destiny is not "lost at sea"; it is **Awaiting Retrieval.** The Marine Vaults are not "Permanent Residences" for your blessings they are "Temporary Holdings" that must be emptied today. Strike the Gavel and authorize the "Angelic Recovery Teams" to descend and bring up your cargo!

The Executive Decree:

"I stand in the Court of Heaven as a Governor and I issue an **Executive Repossession Order!** I address the Marine Kingdom and the 'Belly of the Deep': **Vomit up my Destiny!** I repossess my Marital Honey, my Financial Oil, and the 'Manuscripts of my Spirit.' I break the 'Seals of the Vault' by the Blood of the Lamb! I demand a **sevenfold restitution** for every year the locust of fornication siphoned my virtue. I command the 'Angelic Recovery Teams' to empty the underwater warehouses of my bloodline! My future is no longer submerged; it is **Surface Bound and Manifesting Now, In The name of Jesus!"**

Chapter 12: The Standard of Holiness

The Quality of a True Believer: Living Without Compromise

In the administrative manual of the Kingdom, **Holiness** is not a religious suggestion; it is the **Governor's Primary Policy**. It is the "Structural Integrity" of the believer. While the world defines a believer by "attendance" or "vocal confession," the Kingdom defines a believer by their **Lack of Mixture**. To live without compromise is to ensure that your "Yes" to God is not diluted by a "Maybe" to the culture. It is the quality of a vessel that is so "Full of Light" that the Marine Kingdom finds no "Dark Pocket" to attach a legal claim.

Holiness as "Judicial Weight" (2Corinthians 7:1)

Therefore, having these promises, beloved, let us cleanse ourselves from all filthiness of the flesh and spirit, perfecting holiness in the fear of God."

The Perfecting Process: Holiness is the "Drying Phase" of your foundation. It is the constant removal of "Filthiness" (the saltwater of the past) until the vessel can hold the **Kavod** (the Weighty Glory) of God.

The Weight of Authority: A compromised believer is "Spiritually Light" , they are easily blown away by the "Waves of the Sea." But a holy believer carries **Judicial Weight**. When you speak a decree over your marriage, the spirit realm obeys because it recognizes that there is no "Contraband" in your hands.

The "No Compromise" Boundary (Proverbs 4:25-27)

"Let your eyes look straight ahead... Ponder the path of your feet, and let all your ways be established. Do not turn to the right or the left; remove your foot from evil."

The Straight Path: Living without compromise means the "Foundational Crack" has been sutured. You no longer "negotiate" with the Mother of Harlots. You don't ask, "How far can I go before it's a sin?" Instead, you ask, "How holy can I be to reflect the King?"

The Elimination of the "Gray Zone": The Marine Kingdom thrives in the "Gray Zone", that area of life where you are "mostly" Christian but "partially" worldly. Holiness eliminates the Gray Zone, turning your estate into a **"High Contrast Territory"** where light and dark are clearly defined.

The Quality of "Incorruptibility" (1 Peter 1:15-16)

"But as He who called you is holy, you also be holy in all your conduct, because it is written, 'Be holy, for I am holy.'"

The Standard of the Original: As a Governor, your "Technical Manual" must match the "Original Blueprint" of the King. If the King does not compromise, His Ambassadors cannot afford to.

Conduct as Policy: Holiness is not just what you *don't* do; it is the **Quality of your Conduct**. It is the way you handle your manuscripts, the way you treat your future spouse, and the way you manage your 48-hour fasts. It is an "All Encompassing" standard that leaves no room for "Secret Altars."

The "Dry Ground" Advantage

Living without compromise provides a **Strategic Advantage** in the spirit realm.

The Repulsion of the Aquatic: Just as certain materials are waterproof, a holy life is **"Demon Proof."** The toxins of the Deep cannot stick to a surface that is coated in the "Oil of Consecration."

The Unbroken Signal: Compromise creates "Static" in your prophetic hearing. A holy life provides a "Clear Signal," allowing you to receive the "Technical Manuals" and "Governor's Verdicts" from the Throne Room with 100% accuracy.

The "White Garment" Mandate (Ecclesiastes 9:8)
"Let your garments be always white..."
The Maintenance of Purity: True holiness is a **Daily Administrative Task**. It is the "Daily Bath" in the Word. It is the refusal to let even a "Spot" of the world's philosophy, like "Normalizing Evil", touch your garment.
The Readiness for the future Union: You are preparing for a "Marriage that Must Hold." Only a "White Garment" can survive the intensity of a God ordained covenant. Your holiness is your **Wedding Preparation**.

The Governor's Verdict:
Compromise is the "Slow Leak" that sinks the ship. Holiness is the "Hull" that keeps the ship afloat in the midst of the Deep. You are a True Believer not because you are perfect, but because you are **Uncompromisingly Pursuing the Standard of the King.** Strike the Gavel and declare that the "Season of Mixture" is officially over!

The Executive Decree:
"I stand as a Governor of Zion, and I embrace the **Standard Of Holiness!** I renounce every 'Gray Zone' and every 'Negotiation' with the culture of compromise. I declare that my body, my mind, and my Mandate are **Off Limits** to the Mother of Harlots! I receive the 'Judicial Weight' of the Spirit. I am not a 'Light Vessel' tossed by the waves; I am an 'Incorruptible Estate' built on the Rock! I apply the 'Oil of Consecration' to my life daily. I am holy because my King is holy, and I shall walk in 'Dry Ground' authority all the days of my life, **In the Name of Jesus!"**

The 7 Dimensions of The Spirit of The Lord: Operating in Full Spiritual Capacity (Isaiah 11:2)

In the administrative governance of the Kingdom, the **Spirit of the Lord** is the "Chief Executive" of your internal estate. To write technical manuals, govern a marriage, or dismantle marine altars, a Governor cannot rely on human intellect alone. You must operate in the **Full Spiritual Capacity** of the Seven Fold Spirit. This is the "Engine of Zion" that empowers you to rule over the "Deep" and establish the "Governor's Verdict".

1. The Spirit of the LORD (The Center Stem)

This is the **Spirit of Sovereignty**. It is the "Kavod" (Weight) of God's own Presence.

The Judicial Authority: This dimension gives you the right to issue decrees. When the Spirit of the LORD rests upon you, you don't speak as a "victim" of your past; you speak as a **Plenipotentiary** (a representative with full power) of the King.

The Foundation: This is the "Dry Ground" upon which all other dimensions sit.

2. The Spirit of WISDOM

Wisdom is the **Supernatural Intelligence** required for "Kingdom Construction."

The Structural Integrity: Wisdom is what allows you to see the "Foundational Cracks" before the building collapses. In your marriage, Wisdom will be the "Architect" that ensures the house is built on the Rock.

The Technical Manuals: You cannot write the *Governor's Verdict* without this dimension; it provides the "How To" for complex spiritual problems.

3. The Spirit of UNDERSTANDING

Understanding is the **Analytical Faculty** of the Spirit.

The Discernment of the Deep: While Wisdom gives you the plan, Understanding gives you the "Insight" to see through the "Marine Fog." It allows you to look at a "Modern Relationship" and see the "Invisible Covenant" hiding beneath the surface.

The Blueprint Reader: It translates the mysteries of God into a "Technical Manual" that others can follow.

4. The Spirit of COUNSEL

Counsel is the **Strategic Planning** dimension of the Spirit.

The War Room: In the spirit realm, this is your "Military Strategy." Counsel tells you *when* to fast 48 hours and *how* to strike the Gavel against a specific Spirit Spouse.

The Decision Maker: It eliminates the "Normalizing of Evil" by providing the King's specific advice for every dilemma, ensuring you never have to "Negotiate with the Deep."

5. The Spirit of MIGHT

Might is the **Administrative Power** and "Executive Force."

The Enforcement of the Verdict: Counsel gives you the strategy, but Might gives you the **Strength to Execute** it. It is the "Resisting Power" that allows you to stand without compromise when the "Mother of Harlots" offers her wine.

The Structural Strength: It provides the "Muscle" to pull down altars and dismantle legal demonic claims.

6. The Spirit of KNOWLEDGE

Knowledge is **Experiential Intimacy** and "Data Acquisition" from the Throne.

The Intelligence Report: This dimension gives you "Classified Information" about your bloodline, your future, and the "Cargo at the bottom of the sea."

The Eraser of Ignorance: Hosea 4:6 says people are destroyed for lack of knowledge. This Spirit ensures your "Registry" is clean because you *know* the Truth that sets the estate free.

7. The Spirit of the FEAR OF THE LORD

This is the **Regulator** of the entire Seven Fold System.

The Safety Valve: Just as we discussed in the beginning, this is the "Missing Component." It keeps the Governor from "Compromise."

The Clean Filter: It ensures that your wisdom and power are used for the King's glory and not for the "Flesh." It is the "Beginning of Wisdom" and the "Guardian of the Gate."

The Governor's Verdict:

To operate in "Full Spiritual Capacity" is to have all seven dimensions "Illuminated" like the Menorah. When these seven lamps are burning in your soul, the Marine Kingdom cannot find a single "Dark Corner" to occupy. You become a **High Frequency Governor** who is "Too Hot" for the Deep to handle.

The Executive Decree:

"I stand in my office as a Governor and I call for the **Full Activation** of the Seven-Fold Spirit of the Lord! I receive the Spirit of the **Lord** to govern my estate. I receive **Wisdom** to build my Marriage. I receive **Understanding** to see through the 'Marine Fog.' I receive **Counsel** for my technical manuals. I receive MIGHT to dismantle every altar! I receive **Knowledge** to recover my hijacked cargo. And I receive the **Fear of the Lord** to regulate my soul in holiness. I am operating at Full Capacity, and I refuse to be a 'Light Vessel' anymore! I am Weighted, I am Oiled, and I am **Ready, In the Name of Jesus!"**

Part V: The Call to The New Generation

Chapter 13: Arise and wake up

Gathering the Conferences: Teaching the Truth the Church Has Normalized

In the final administrative phase of your mandate, the Governor moves from "Personal Restoration" to **"Generational Mobilization."** The "Gathering of Conferences" is not for the sake of religious gathering; it is a **Judicial Summit** designed to deprogram a generation that has been fed the "Sedative of Normalization." The Church has largely traded the "Gavel of Truth" for the "Cushion of Comfort," leading to a generation of believers who are born again in spirit but remain **Marine Annexed** in their foundations.

The Convocation of the "Remnant Governors" (Joel 2:15-16)

"Blow the trumpet in Zion, consecrate a fast, call a sacred assembly; gather the people, sanctify the congregation, assemble the elders, gather the children and nursing babes; let the bridegroom go out from his chamber, and the bride from her dressing room."

Breaking the "Privacy" Lie: Modern culture says your sexual life is "private." The Conference of Truth declares it is **"Judicial."** * **The Intergenerational Mandate:** This gathering is for everyone, from the "Elder" whose foundation is crumbling to the "Nursing Babe" whose destiny is being traded. You are gathering them to **Sanctify the Congregation** by exposing the "Invisible Covenants" that the modern pulpit is too afraid to mention.

Exposing the "Lease Agreements" of the Deep

The Church has normalized "Forgiveness without Deliverance."

The Missing Teaching: Most conferences focus on "Motivation." , Prosperity" Your conference must focus on **"Mechanics."** You must teach the "Mechanics of the Altar" and the "Law of the One Flesh Merger."

The Deprogramming: You are teaching them that "Feeling Forgiven" is not the same as being "Judicially Cleared." You are showing them how to identify the "Rattle of the Spirit Spouse" in their marriages and how to sue for the "Repossession of their Sunken Cargo."

The "Standard of the 144,000" (Revelation14:4)

"These are the ones who were not defiled with women, for they are virgins. These are the ones who follow the Lamb wherever He goes."

Restoring the "Aesthetic of Purity": The "Normalized Evil" has made virginity look like "Weakness" and holiness look like "Legalism." Your conferences must restore the **Spiritual Royalty** associated with purity.

The New Virginity: You must teach the "Protocol of the Cleansing Bath," showing that through the Blood of Jesus, a "Soiled Generation" can be restored to a state of **Judicial Virginity**, becoming a "Clean Generation" that can stand on the Hill of the Lord.

Shifting from "Church" to "Chancery"

A "Chancery" is a court of equity and conscience.

The Judicial Atmosphere: The atmosphere of your conferences must not be "Emotional Excitement," but **"Administrative Weight."** When people walk in, they should feel the "Fear of the Lord" (The Regulator) and the "Might of the Spirit."

The Gavel Activation: You are teaching every young person how to operate their own Gavel. You are training them to be **Governors of their own Estates**, so they can go home and dismantle the altars of their fathers just like "Gideon".

The Wake up Call: The Midnight Cry (Matthew 25:6)
"And at midnight a cry was heard: 'Behold, the bridegroom is coming; go out to meet him!'"
The Urgency of this Era: You are sounding the alarm that the "Marriage Window" is opening, but only for those whose lamps are "Oiled" and whose vessels are "Dry."
Gathering the "Cultural Carriers": You are looking for the "Cultural Carriers" those who will take this "Technical Manual" into the media, the government, and the schools to stop the "National Judgment" before it consumes the city.

The Governor's Verdict
The "Normalized Evil" ends when the **Truth is Systematized.** These conferences are the "Assembly Lines" for a new kind of believer, one who is uncompromised, unpolluted, and fully operational in the Seven Dimensions of the Spirit. You are not just "Waking Up" a generation; you are **Inaugurating an Army.**

The Executive Decree:
"I stand as a Governor of the New Generation and I sound the **Alarm in Zion!** I authorize the 'Gathering of the Conferences' to teach the Truth that has been buried under compromise. I strike the Gavel against the 'Spirit of Slumber' and the 'Sedative of Normalization.' I declare that a generation is **Waking Up** to their judicial authority! We are de registering from the Marine Kingdom and re registering in the Kingdom of Light. We are the 'Clean Generation' that will repair the breach. The 'Mother of Harlots' loses her grip on our youth **Today**! We are Rising, we are Governing, and we are **Ready, In The Name Of Jesus!"**

The Importance of Virginity: Defining Purity in a Defiled World

In the spiritual jurisprudence of the Kingdom, **Virginity** is far more than a physical condition; it is a **Judicial Status**. While the world views it as a "social construct" or an "outdated burden," the Governor recognizes it as the **Ultimate Seal of an Unbroken Estate**. To be a virgin spiritually and physically is to have a foundation that has never been "Wet" with the illegal fluids of the Deep. It is the gold standard of a **Clean Generation** and the highest level of "Structural Integrity" a believer can bring into Marital Covenant.

The Judicial Seal of Ownership (Song of Solomon 4:12)

"A garden enclosed is my sister, my spouse; a spring shut up, a fountain sealed."

The Enclosed Garden: Virginity is a "No Entry" sign to the Marine Kingdom. It represents a garden whose gates have never been breached by a "Foreigner."

The Sealed Fountain: In the spirit realm, a "Seal" is a mark of **Sovereign Ownership**. When a vessel is sealed, it indicates that no "Trade" has occurred with the Mother of Harlots. The "Marital Honey" is intact, and the "Prophetic Oil" is unpolluted. This "Seal" acts as a natural repellent to the toxins of previous unions.

The Strength of the "Single Bond" Foundation

As a **Governor**, you know that the "Two become One"(1 Corinthians 6:16).

The Clarity of the Merger: When two virgins marry, they are performing a **Single Bond Merger**. There are no "Third Party Signals," no "Residual Personalities," and no "Marine Wardens" claiming seniority.

The Structural Advantage: A foundation built by two virgins is "Instantly Set." There is no need for years of "Scraping the Walls" or

"Dismantling Altars" because no altars were ever built. This marriage starts with a **Full Reservoir of Peace**, which is the "Standard of Excellence" for the New Generation.

Virginity as "Spiritual Capital" (Revelation 14:4)

"These are the ones who were not defiled with women, for they are virgins... These were redeemed from among men, being first fruits to God and to the Lamb."

The First fruits Power: There is a specific "Judicial Weight" (Kavod) assigned to the "First fruits." In the Court of Heaven, the testimony of a virgin carries a frequency that "The Deep" cannot mimic.

The Ransom Value: Purity is **Spiritual Capital**. It provides the "Currency" needed to buy back the territory of your city and nation. A "Clean Generation" doesn't just "resist" the devil; they **Bankrupt** his influence by refusing to trade in his market.

Defining the "New Virginity" (The Restoration of the Seal)

Because we live in a defiled world, the Governor must also teach the **"Judicial Restoration of Purity."**

Beyond the Physical: While physical virginity is the "Original Blueprint," God provides a protocol for **Secondary Virginity**. This is for the "Restored Governor" who has gone through the "Cleansing Bath" and the "Judicial Annulment" of past mergers.

The "Virginity of the Soul": Through the Blood of Jesus, your soul can be "Re Sealed." The Just Judge can issue a **"Certificate of Purity,"** declaring that your past "Illegal Leases" are so completely blotted out that you stand before Him as a "Chaste Virgin" (2Corinthians 11:2).

The Aesthetic of Holiness vs. The Culture of Exposure

The Protection of the Vessel: In a world that demands "Exposure" (normalization of evil, immodesty, sexual openness), the Governor chooses **"Enclosure."** * **The Royal Standard:** Virginity is the "Royal Robe" of the Kingdom. It is the refusal to let the "Mother of Harlots" see what is reserved for the King. It is the preservation of the "Technical Manual" of your body until the **Governor's Verdict** is signed and sealed in marriage.

The Governor's Verdict

Virginity is not the "absence of experience"; it is the **presence of Consecration.** It is the decision to keep your foundation "Bone Dry" until the "Rightful Owner" arrives. Whether you are holding your original seal or you have been "Judicially Restored" in the Cleansing Bath, you must guard your purity as the **Primary Asset** of your estate.

The Executive Decree:

"I stand as a Governor of the Clean Generation and I declare the **Restoration of The Standard of Purity!** I renounce the lies of a defiled world that mock the beauty of virginity. I declare that my body is a 'Garden Enclosed' and a 'Fountain Sealed' for the King! By the Gavel of the Just Judge, I receive my 'Judicial Seal' either preserved or restored by the Blood of the Lamb. I refuse to trade my virtue in the Marine Markets! I am a First fruit to God, and I am preparing my estate for my Marriage that is Holy, Weighted, and Unbroken, **In The name of Jesus!"**

Chapter 14: Training The Bloodline

Train Up a Child": Building a Generation That Will Not Depart (Proverbs 22:6)

In the judicial administration of a Governor's estate, **Training** is not merely "parenting", it is the **Systematic Transfer of Structural Integrity**. To "Train up a child in the way he should go" is to build a "Foundational Levee" in their soul that protects them from the "Marine Inundation" of the culture. As you prepare for your **Marriage**, you must recognize that your children will not just inherit your DNA; they will inherit your **Altars**. Training is the process of ensuring that the "Technical Manual" of Holiness is written on their hearts before the "Mother of Harlots" attempts to draft her own.

The Judicial Definition of "Training" (Proverbs 22:6)

"Train up a child in the way he should go, and when he is old, he will not depart from it."

Narrowing the Path: "initiate," or "dedicate." The children early there is nothing like is too early start teaching them bold ways of the Lord, without compromise.

The Taste of Zion: Training is **"Palate Education."** You are teaching your children to "Taste" the sweetness of the Dry Ground so that the "Saltwater" of the Marine Kingdom tastes like poison to them.

Building the "Internal Governor"

Training is the transition from **External Control** to **Internal Governance**.

The Manual of Conduct: You are not just teaching "rules"; you are teaching the **"Governor's Verdict."** You are explaining the *why* behind the *what*. When a child understands the "Law of the One Flesh Merger" and the "Toxins of the Deep," they don't avoid fornication out of fear of punishment, but out of a **Judicial Respect** for their own vessel.

The Self Cleaning Foundation: A well trained child has a "Self-Correcting" mechanism. When they encounter "Normalized Evil" at school or in the media, their internal "Spirit of Understanding" sounds an alarm, and they voluntarily move back to the Rock.

The Altar of the Home: The Training Ground

The home is the **Primary Chancery (Court)** where the child learns the protocols of the Kingdom.

The Atmosphere of the Dry Ground: If the parents have "Rattling Spirits" or "Hidden Rivalries," the training will be compromised. A child can sense "Marine Moisture" in a home. Training requires a **Clear Atmosphere** where the "Fear of the Lord" (The Regulator) is the primary resident.

The 7 Dimensions at the Dinner Table: Training involves activating the Seven Fold Spirit in the child. You teach them to seek **Counsel** from the Spirit, to exercise **Might** over their impulses, and to walk in the **Knowledge** of their identity as Royal Priests.

Protecting the "Seed" from Legacy Leakage

As discussed in Chapter 8, "Iniquity" is a generational leak. Training is the **"Maintenance Protocol"** that keeps the leak from re opening.

The Firewall of the Word: By saturating the child in the "Liquid Word," you are creating a **Spiritual Firewall**. Even if they are surrounded by a "Defiled World," the fire of the Word inside them prevents the "Marine Wardens" from finding an entry point.

The Vision: You must parent with the **Future Marriage of the Child** in mind. You are training them today so that their "Marriage of 2050" will hold, just as your "Marriage of 2026" must hold.

The Result: A Generation That "Will Not Depart"
The promise is judicial: *"He will not depart from it."*
The Law of Habituation: When a foundation is poured correctly and allowed to "Set" in the Light, it becomes an irreversible structure.
The Remnant Legacy: A trained child becomes a "Cultural Carrier." They carry the "Technical Manuals" you have written into the next generation, ensuring that the **Bloodline of Purity** continues until the King returns.

The Governor's Verdict
To train a child is to **Govern the Future**. You are not raising "kids"; you are raising **Kingdom Ambassadors**. Do not leave their palate to be educated by the "Mother of Harlots." Rub the "Honey of the Word" on their souls today!

The Executive Decree:
"I stand as a Governor over my Bloodline and I embrace the **Mandate to Train!** I declare that my children (born and unborn) shall be initiated into the 'Way of the Rock.' I strike the Gavel against every 'Cultural Influencer' trying to educate their palates with the saltwater of the Deep. I decree that my home is a 'Training Chancery' where the Seven Fold Spirit of the Lord resides. My seed shall be 'Great in the Earth,' and they shall Never depart from the path of Holiness. They are the 'Clean Generation,' and their foundations are **Dry and Unbreakable, In the name of Jesus!"**

Establishing The New Bloodline: A Generation That Fears the Almighty
In the judicial realm of the Kingdom, a **Bloodline** is more than a biological sequence; it is a **Spiritual Pipeline** that carries either the "Toxins of the Deep" or the "Fire of the Altar." Establishing a *New*

Bloodline is the ultimate executive act of a Governor. It is the process of "Re authoring" your lineage so that the generations following your union do not inherit a "Foundational Crack," but rather a **Registry of Righteousness.** This is the creation of a "New Species" of family one that is governed by the **Fear of the Almighty.**

The Judicial "Cut-Off" and Re-Grafting (Romans11:24)

To establish a new bloodline, there must first be a **Judicial Severance** from the old one.

The Suture of the Past: You are the "Intergenerational Surgeon." By the Gavel, you are "Cutting the Cord" that connected your loins to the fornications and "Marine Covenants" of your ancestors.

The New Root: You are being re grafted into the **Root of Jesse**. When you establish this new bloodline, your children are no longer "Products of the Deep"; they are "Offshoots of Zion." Their spiritual DNA is re coded with the **Fear of the Lord**, which acts as a permanent "Antibody" against the normalized evils of the world.

The Fear of the Lord as a "Bloodline Regulator"

The "Fear of the Almighty" is not terror; it is a **Judicial Awareness** of God's holiness.

The Internal Compass: In the New Bloodline, the "Fear of the Lord" is the primary **Regulatory System**. It is the "Moral Law" written into the very pulse of the generation.

The Immunity System: Just as the body has an immune system to fight viruses, the Fear of the Lord in the bloodline fights the "Virus of Compromise." A child born into this new bloodline will feel an "Internal Repulsion" toward the Mother of Harlots because their "Blood" recognizes the King.

The Registry of the "First Generation"

You are the **Foundational Parent**. Your marriage is the "Year Zero" for this New Bloodline.

The Erasure of the Lien: Every debt of the past is settled. This new generation starts with a **"Positive Balance"** in the Court of Heaven. They do not start by "fighting" their parents' demons; they start by **"Occupying"** their parents' victories.

The Wealth of Purity: This bloodline carries "Spiritual Capital." Because the foundation is "Dry," the blessings of Deuteronomy 28 are not "leaked" through sexual sin; they are **Accumulated**. The "Honey" of the marriage is preserved to fuel the purpose of the children.

Training the "Prophetic DNA" (Psalm 112:1-2)

"Praise the Lord! Blessed is the man who fears the Lord... His descendants will be mighty on earth; the generation of the upright will be blessed."

The Mighty Seed: The New Bloodline produces "Mighty Descendants" individuals who are not "Fragile" in the face of national judgment.

The Sharpness of the Seed: Because their "Foundational Sight" is not blurred by the Marine Fog of their parents' past, these children will have **High Definition Prophetic Sight**. They will see the "Technical Manuals" of the next century with absolute clarity.

The "Covenant of Salt" (2Chronicles13:5)

A New Bloodline is sealed with a **Covenant of Salt**, an incorruptible and permanent agreement.

The Preservative Quality: Just as salt prevents decay, the Fear of the Lord in your new bloodline prevents the "Rot of the Culture" from entering your home.

The Eternal Gavel: You are establishing a bloodline that will still be "Dry and Set" when the King returns. This is the **Legacy of the Governor**.

The Governor's Verdict

The "Old Bloodline" ends at the Cross; the "New Bloodline" begins at the **Altar of your 2026 Covenant.** You are not just getting married; you are **Inaugurating a Dynasty of Purity.** Strike the Gavel and declare that the "Registry of the Grave" is closed, and the "Registry of the Almighty" is open for your seed!

The Executive Decree:
"I stand as a Governor and I issue an **Executive Inauguration** of my New Bloodline! I strike the Gavel against every generational leak and every marine tracking system. By the Blood of the Lamb, I RE **Code** my DNA and the DNA of my future seed with the **Fear Of The Almighty!** My 2026 marriage is 'Year Zero' of a Dynasty of Light. My children shall not fight my battles; they shall possess my gates! I declare that my lineage is a 'Salt Covenant', incorruptible, unpolluted, and mighty in the earth. The 'Mother of Harlots' has no share in my posterity! We are the 'Clean Generation,' and we belong to the King, **In The Name Of Jesus!"**

Final Prayers: The Executive Warfare Protocol

Phase I: Confession, Repentance, and Foundational Dismantling

1. **The Verdict of Annulment**

Decree: "I judicially confess every act of fornication as Foundational Treason. By the Blood of the Lamb, I demand a Total Annulment of every soul-tie formed in the Deep."

Scripture: "If we confess our sins, He is faithful and just to forgive us our sins and to cleanse us from all unrighteousness." (**1 John 1:9**)

2. **Dismantling the Marine Altar**

Decree: "I command the 'Foundation Stones' of harlotry to be uprooted and cast into the fire. The site is **Cleared** for my holy Marital Covenant."

Scripture: "Pull down the altar of Baal that your father has... and build an altar to the Lord your God on top of this rock." (**Judges 6:25-26**)

3. **Breaking the "Writ of Seniority"**

Decree: "I renounce every 'Spirit Spouse' and 'Marine Warden.' Your lease is **expired**. I evict every spiritual squatter today."

Scripture: "Having canceled the charge of our legal indebtedness, which stood against us and condemned us; he has taken it away, nailing it to the cross." (**Colossians 2:14**)

4. **Purging the "Liquid Toxins"**

Decree: "I call for the Cleansing Bath of the Word to flush my subconscious. I neutralize the 'Marine Fog' that blurred my prophetic sharpness."

Scripture: "That He might sanctify and cleanse her with the washing of water by the word." (**Ephesians 5:26**)

5. **The Suture of the Bloodline**

Decree: "I suture every 'Generational Leak' created by sexual sin. I disconnect my future children from the 'Genetic Pager' of the Deep."

Scripture: "Christ has redeemed us from the curse of the law, having become a curse for us." (**Galatians 3:13**)

Phase II: Breaking Suicidal Attachments and Death Covenants

6. **The Stay of Execution**

Decree: "I strike the Gavel against every Spirit of Death that traveled through sexual chains. I shall not expire before my mandate is fulfilled."

Scripture: "I shall not die, but live, and declare the works of the Lord." (**Psalm 118:17**)

7. **Draining the Saltwater**

Decree: "I command the 'Liquid Sorrow' and 'Marine Darkness' in my mind to be drained. I breathe in the Ruach of God and I choose life."

Scripture: "To give them beauty for ashes, the oil of joy for mourning, the garment of praise for the spirit of heaviness." (**Isaiah 61:3**)

8. **Breaking the "Grave Registry"**

Decree: "I de-register my name from the 'Archives of the Grave.' My body is a Temple of Life, not a highway to death."

Scripture: "Your covenant with death will be annulled, and your agreement with Sheol will not stand." (**Isaiah 28:18**)

Phase III: Marital Restoration and the Mandate

9. **The Eviction of "Married Strangers"**

Decree: "I silence the 'Rattle' of the Spirit Spouse. My marriage bed is a Toxin-Free Zone. No third party is permitted in my union."

Scripture: "Marriage is honorable among all, and the bed undefiled; but fornicators and adulterers God will judge." (**Hebrews 13:4**)

10. **Repossessing the "Marital Honey"**

Decree: "I command the Marine Vaults to vomit up my capacity for delight. I repossess the 'Honey' siphoned through past harlotry."

Scripture: "He swallows down riches and vomits them up again; God will cast them out of his belly." (**Job 20:15**)

11. **Securing the "Marriage that Must Hold"**

Decree: "I establish my marriage on the Dry Ground of the Rock. I strike the Gavel against the 'Serpent of Divorce' and the 'Harvest of Chaos.'

Scripture: "What God has joined together, let not man [or spirit] separate." (**Matthew 19:6**)

12. **The Restoration of Virginity**

Decree: "I receive my Judicial Seal of Purity. I am not 'Soiled Goods'; I am a sanctified Governor and a chaste virgin."

Scripture: "For I have betrothed you to one husband, that I may present you as a chaste virgin to Christ." (**2 Corinthians 11:2**)

Phase IV: Repossessing Destiny, Wealth, and Manuscripts

13. **Retrieving the "Prophetic Cargo"**

Decree: "I authorize Angelic Recovery Teams to retrieve my 'Technical Manuals' and my 'Manuscripts' from the Marine Vaults."

Scripture: "I will give you the treasures of darkness and hidden riches of secret places." (**Isaiah 45:3**)

14. **The Wealth Transfer Decree:** "I command the 'Wealth of the Seas' siphoned from my bloodline to be returned sevenfold! I reverse the siphoning pipe."

Scripture: "If the thief is found, he must restore sevenfold; he may have to give up all the substance of his house." (**Proverbs 6:31**)

15. **Activating the 7 Dimensions**

Decree: "I call for the Full Activation of the Seven-Fold Spirit! I receive Wisdom, Understanding, Counsel, Might, Knowledge, and the Fear of the Lord."

Scripture: "The Spirit of the Lord shall rest upon him, the Spirit of wisdom and understanding, the Spirit of counsel and might, the Spirit of knowledge and of the fear of the Lord." (**Isaiah 11:2**)

Phase V: National Judgment and the New Bloodline

16. **Striking "Normalized Evil"**

Decree: "I strike the Gavel against the 'Normalization of Abomination.' I declare that I am part of the Clean Generation."

Scripture: "And do not be conformed to this world, but be transformed by the renewing of your mind." (**Romans 12:2**)

17. **Closing the "Gate of Abortion"**

Decree: "I renounce the blood debt of abortion in my nation and bloodline. The Blood of the Covenant speaks better things."

Scripture: "To Jesus the mediator of a new covenant, and to the sprinkled blood that speaks a better word than the blood of Abel." (**Hebrews 12:24**)

18. **Inaugurating the New Bloodline**

Decree: "I inaugurate a New Dynasty for my seed! My children shall not inherit my cracks, but my victories."

Scripture: "His descendants will be mighty on earth; the generation of the upright will be blessed." (**Psalm 112:2**)

19. **The Gathering of the Remnant**

Decree: "I decree that my conferences shall be 'Judicial Summits' of Truth. I command the Spirit of Slumber to break off the youth."

Scripture: "Blow the trumpet in Zion, sanctify a fast, call a solemn assembly: Gather the people, sanctify the congregation." (**Joel 2:15-16**)

20. **The Governor's Final Verdict**

Decree: "I seal these decrees with the Covenant of Salt. My foundation is **Dry, Holy, and Irreversible**. It is finished!"

Scripture: "Should you not know that the Lord God of Israel gave the dominion over Israel to David forever, to him and his sons, by a covenant of salt?" (**2 Chronicles 13:5**)

Conclusion: The Verdict on The Sexual Merger

This final verdict addresses the specific "Foundational Crack" of **Sex Before Marriage**. In the spirit realm, this act was not a mere physical mistake; it was a **Civil War within your Foundation**. By moving into the "One Flesh" merger outside of the "Covenant of Marriage," a legal portal was opened to the Marine Kingdom. However, as a **Governor**, you have now completed the judicial deconstruction of those illegal altars.

The Breaking of the "Illegal Merger"

The conclusion of this matter is the **Total Severance** of every soul tie formed in the bed of fornication. You have moved beyond the "Normalizing of Evil" that the world and a compromised Church have promoted. By identifying these acts as **Legal Entry Points** for the "Mother of Harlots," you have revoked the enemy's right to use your past to blackmail your future. The "Liquid Contract" has been dried by the Fire of the Holy Ghost.

The Restoration of the "Marital Honey"

Sex before marriage is a "Theft of the Future." It siphons the sweetness intended for your holy union and stores it in **Marine Vaults**. The conclusion of your restoration is the **Repossession** of that honey. You are no longer entering your future marriage as "Soiled Goods" or a "Leaky Vessel." Through the **Cleansing Bath**, your "Judicial Virginity" has been restored. You are presenting to your spouse and your King a vessel that is **Sealed and Sanctified**.

The Closure of the Generational Leak

You have recognized that sex before marriage was the "Genetic Pager" used by the Deep to track your bloodline. By the **Gavel of the Spirit**, you have sutured this leak. Your children will not be

"Automatic Debtors" to the marine spirits of your past. You have established a **New Bloodline** where the Fear of the Almighty is the regulator, ensuring that the "Sexually Normalized Evil" of this generation stops at your doorstep.

The Governor's Final Execution

The case of "The Illegal Merger" is now **Closed** in the Court of Heaven. The Judge has seen the Blood; the Governor has struck the Gavel; the Estate is now **Dry Ground.**

The Final Verdict on Purity: "I stand as a Governor and I issue the **Final Verdict** over my sexuality and my foundation! I declare that every 'One Flesh' bond formed before marriage is **Judicially Dissolved**. I refuse the 'Harvest of Chaos' and I reject the 'Spirit of Divorce' birthed from past fornication. I have moved from the 'Wet Foundation' of compromise to the 'Dry Rock' of Holiness. My body is no longer a 'Trading Floor' for the Marine Kingdom; it is the **Private Estate of the King**. I am ready for a marriage built on Purity, Power, and the Seven-Fold Spirit. The past is dead, the debt is paid, and the Governor is in control. **In The Name of Jesus, It Is Finished!**"

About the Author - Dr. Philomena Gerald
Medical Doctor | Intercessor | Author | Kingdom Strategist

Dr. Philomena Gerald is a Medical doctor, Devoted wife and mother, and a Commissioned intercessor with a global mandate for spiritual restoration and deliverance. She is the Founder and visionary leader of *Jesus Deliverance Clinic International Ministries*, a dynamic apostolic hub dedicated to healing, foundational reconstruction, and the enforcement of Kingdom authority.

With a rare integration of medical expertise and deep spiritual insight, Dr. Philomena operates at the intersection of clinical care and spiritual deliverance, addressing both physical conditions and foundational spiritual issues affecting individuals, families, and communities.

Calling & Ministry Assignment

Dr. Philomena is widely recognized as the Convener of the *Midnight Battle Intercessory Prayer*, a strategic and prophetic movement that mobilizes believers to engage in targeted spiritual warfare. This platform emphasizes the execution of divine judgments, referred to as the **"Verdict of the Decree"**, against entrenched powers of darkness.

Her ministry assignment centers on:

- Restoring broken foundations
- Uprooting generational patterns and legal claims
- Equipping believers to function as Governors of Light
- Enforcing Kingdom laws through spiritual intelligence and prayer

Her mission is clear:
To transition the Body of Christ from subjects of circumstance into rulers of spiritual territory through deep foundational deliverance.

The Library of Dr. Philomena Gerald

Strategies for Governance, Deliverance, and Kingdom Authority

Featured Publications:

1. **Deep Foundational Deliverance**
   Secret to Spiritual Warfare: Identifying and uprooting hidden legal claims, ancestral covenants, and ancient cycles of defeat.

2. **Prayer Against Witchcraft: Overruled**
   Dismantling Darkness: Severe warfare prayers and judicial decrees against witchcraft, sorcery, evil altars, and demonic monitoring systems.

3. **Divine Eviction of Addiction**
   Restoring the Temple: Judicial prayers to break addiction, mental oppression, wasting spirits, trauma cycles, and premature death.

4. **Courts of Heaven (Vol. 1): From Defendant to Ruler**
   The Governor's Brief: Transitioning from spiritual victimhood into Kingdom authority through divine legal protocol.

5. **Courts of Heaven (Vol. 2): Silencing the Accuser**
   Securing the Verdict: Enforcing the judgments of Heaven, silencing satanic accusations, and maintaining spiritual victory.

6. **Children Daily Prayer Manual**
   The Next Generation: A 365-day Kingdom training manual for raising spiritual leaders, royal priests, and Kingdom executives.

7. **Sex Before Marriage**
   Foundational Corruption: Breaking soul ties, covenant defilement, lust patterns, and restoring purity, identity, and covenant alignment.

8. **Family Foundational Deliverance**
   Breaking Household Bondage: Exposing inherited patterns, family altars, bloodline afflictions, and ancestral legal rights.

9. **The Praying Mother**
   The Watchwoman's Mantle: Intercessory strategies for mothers to preserve destinies, cover families in prayer, and establish godly bloodlines.

10. **Deliverance from Familiar Spirits**
    Breaking Evil Familiarity: Identifying and destroying monitoring spirits, inherited demonic patterns, spiritual impersonation, and satanic manipulation.

11. **Deliverance from Spirit Spouses**
    Breaking Ungodly Covenants: Deliverance prayers against spiritual marriages, dream pollution, covenant bondage, and marital delay.

Where to Locate & Listen:

You can find these life-changing resources across all major digital and audio platforms:

- **E-Books & Paperbacks:** Available on **Google Books**, **Amazon Kindle**, and **Barnes & Noble**.
- **Audiobooks:** Professionally narrated versions are available on **Apple Books**, **Audible**, and **ACX**.
- **Audio Streaming:** Search for "Dr. Philomena Gerald" on your preferred audiobook provider to listen on the go.

About the Ministry

Dr. Philomena Gerald is a commissioned voice for the restoration of foundations and the enforcement of Kingdom Law.

Primary Ministry: Founder of **Jesus Deliverance Clinic International Ministries**, a global hub for spiritual healing and foundational reconstruction.

The Midnight Call: Convener of the **Midnight Battle Prayer**, a strategic intercession movement that gathers believers monthly to execute the "Verdict of the Decree" against the powers of darkness.

Mission: To transition the Body of Christ from "subjects of circumstance" to "Governors of Light" through deep foundational deliverance.

www.ingramcontent.com/pod-product-compliance
Lightning Source LLC
LaVergne TN
LVHW010949110826
845149LV00015B/3279
* 9 7 9 8 9 9 5 3 8 6 1 7 9 *